for all
the drivers

First English Edition
Printed by Gauvin in Gatineau, Quebec

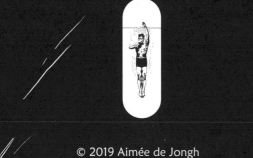

ISBN 978-1-77262-039-9
CIP available from Library and Archives Canada

Conundrum International
Wolfville, Nova Scotia, Canada
www.conundrumpress.com

Distributed in Canada by Litdistco,
distributed in US and internationally by Consortium.

Conundrum Press acknowledges the financial assistance of the Canada Council for the Arts, the Government of Canada, and the Nova Scotia Creative Industries Fund.

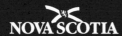

NOVA SCOTIA

Canada Council for the Arts
Conseil des Arts du Canada

Canada

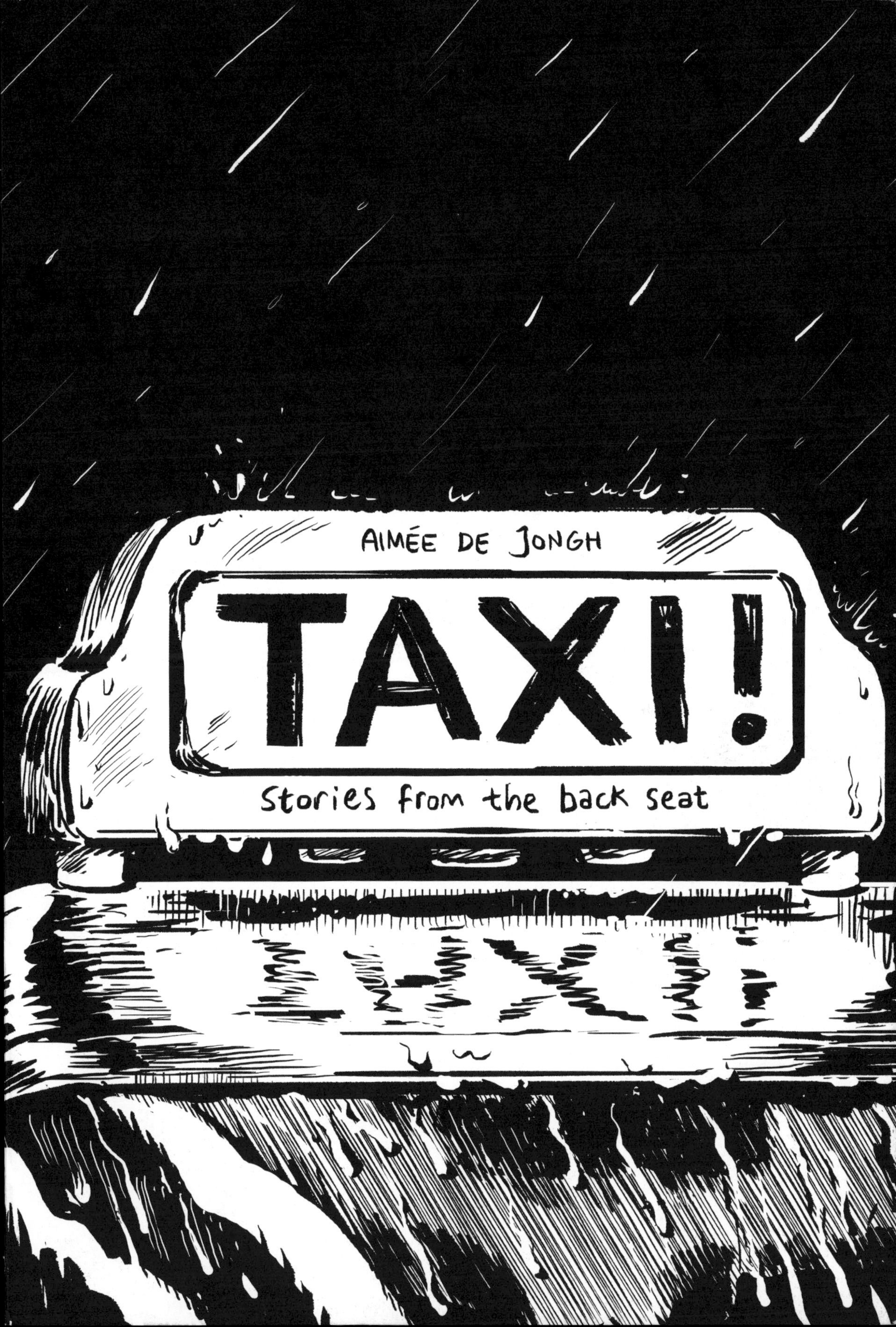
AIMÉE DE JONGH
TAXI!
Stories from the back seat

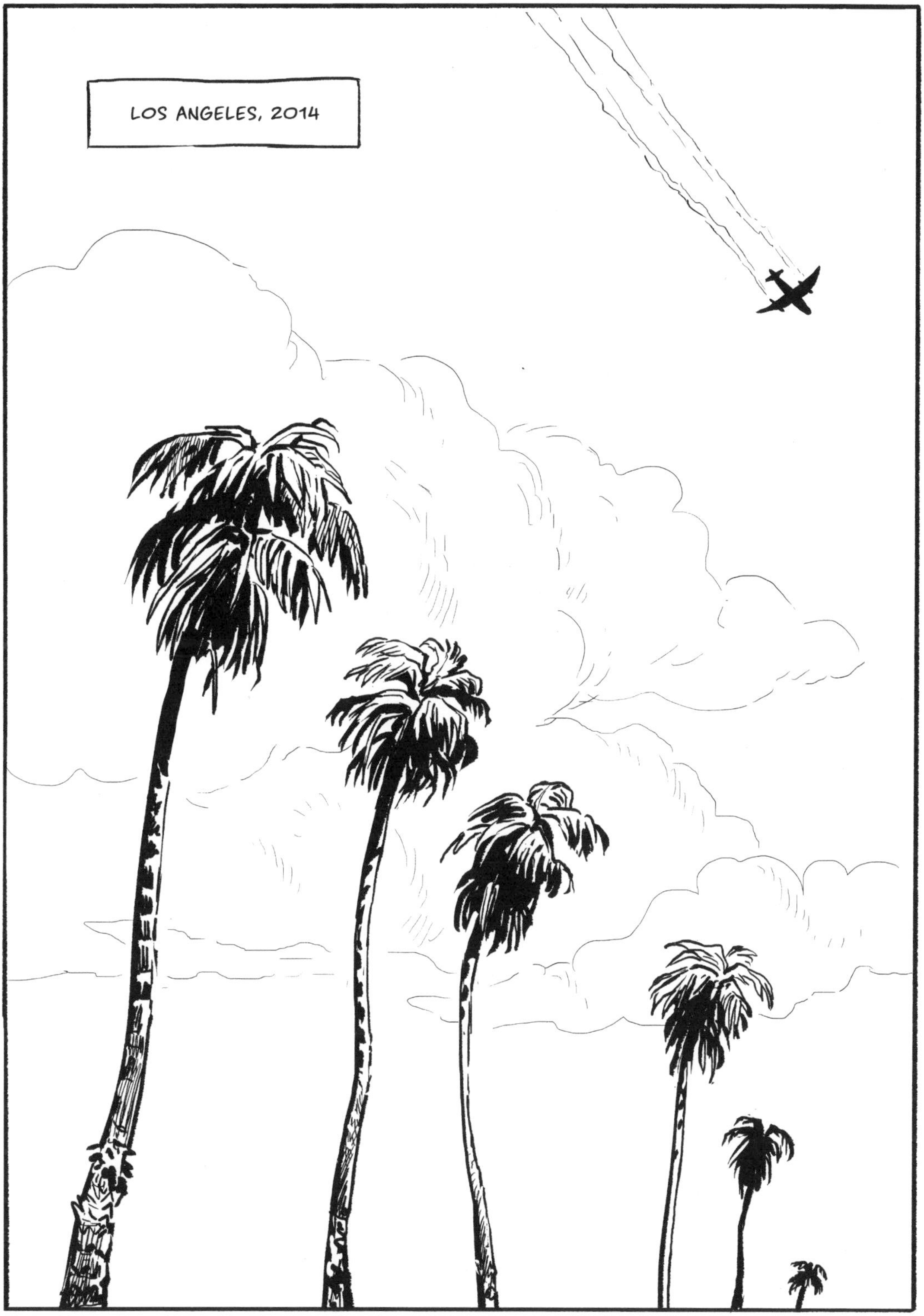
LOS ANGELES, 2014

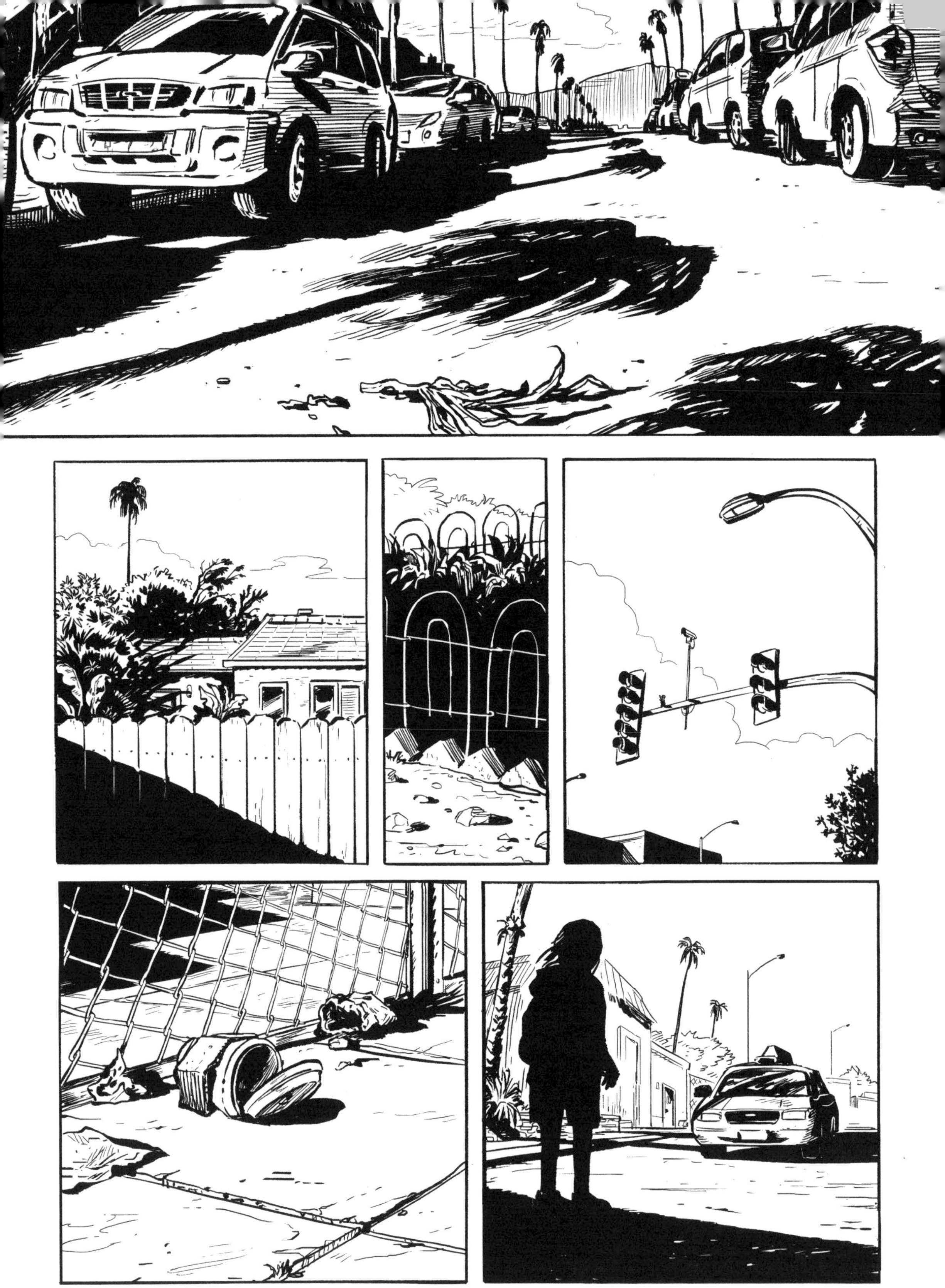

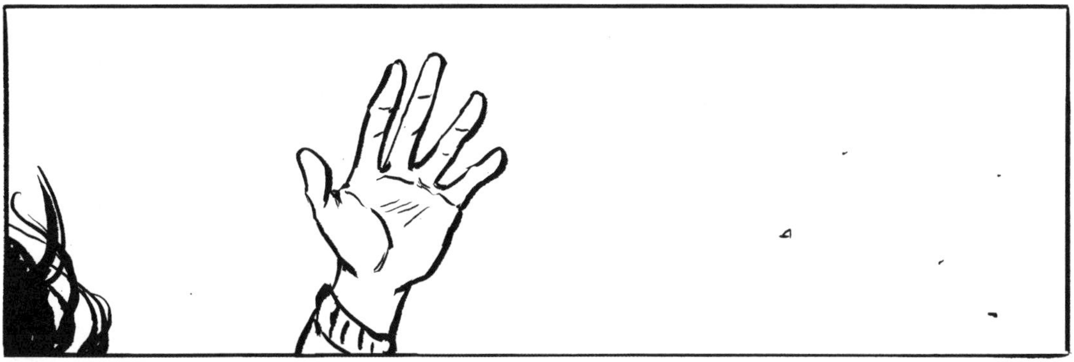

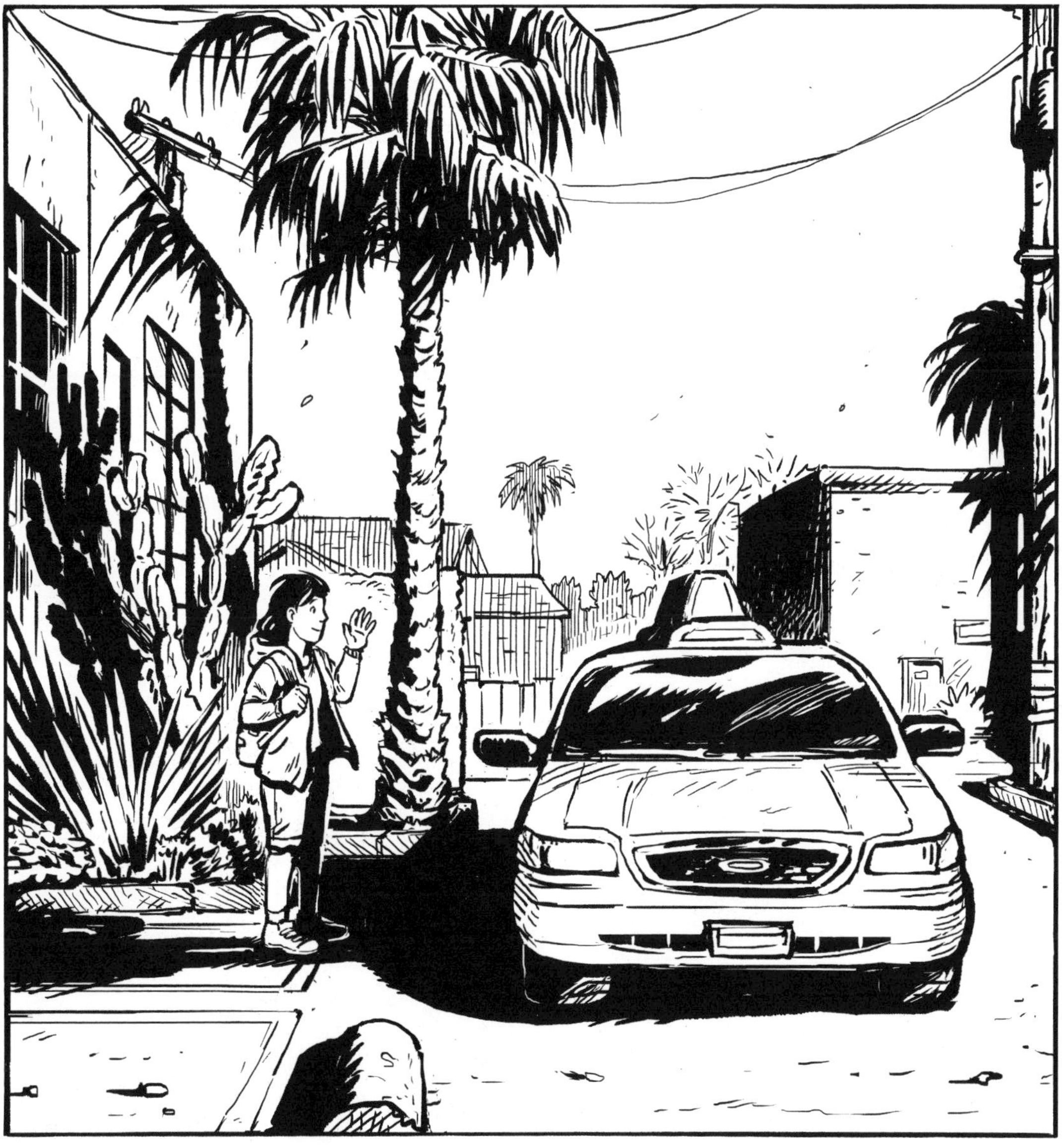

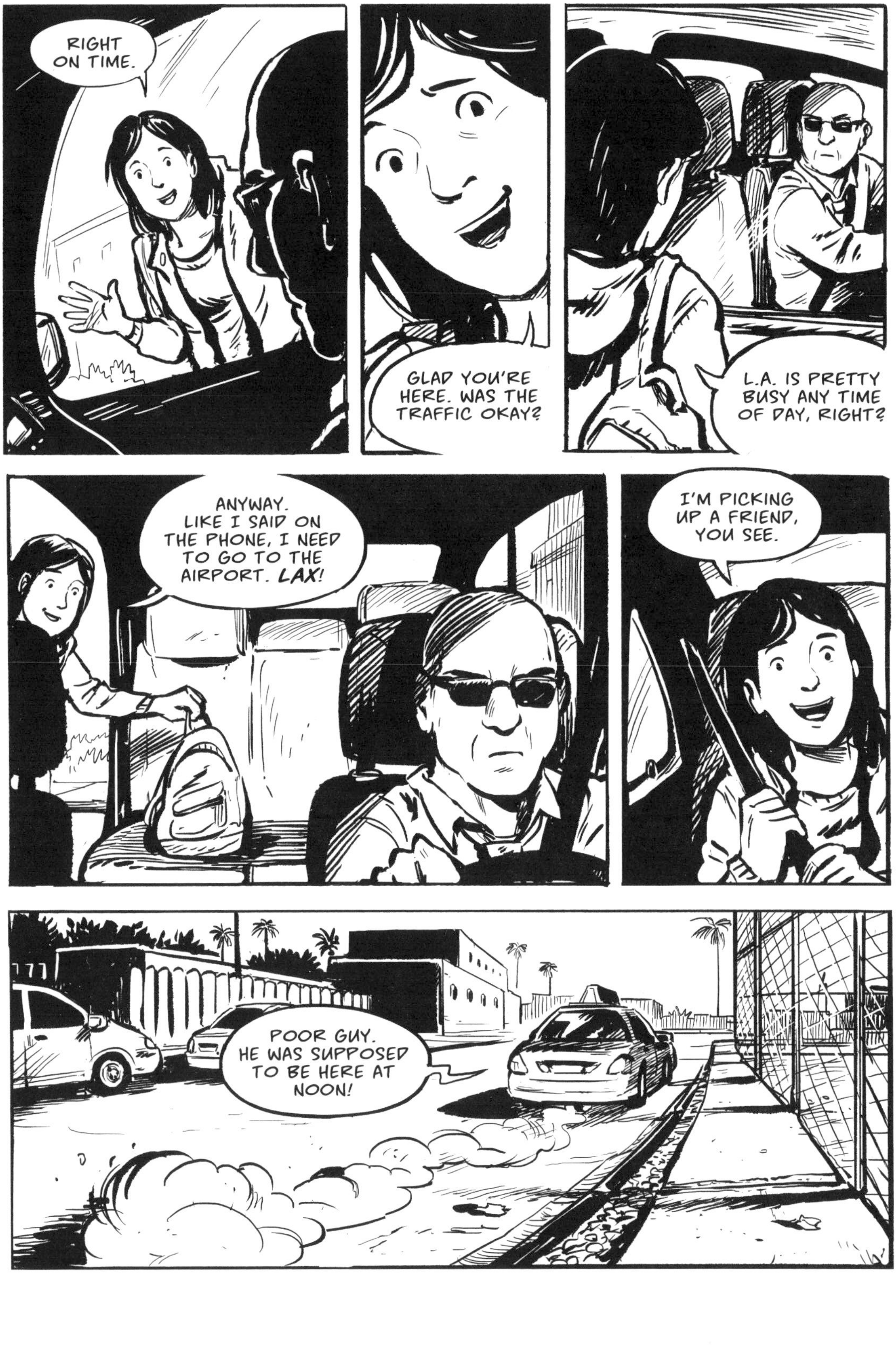
RIGHT ON TIME.
GLAD YOU'RE HERE. WAS THE TRAFFIC OKAY?
L.A. IS PRETTY BUSY ANY TIME OF DAY, RIGHT?
ANYWAY. LIKE I SAID ON THE PHONE, I NEED TO GO TO THE AIRPORT. LAX!
I'M PICKING UP A FRIEND, YOU SEE.
POOR GUY. HE WAS SUPPOSED TO BE HERE AT NOON!

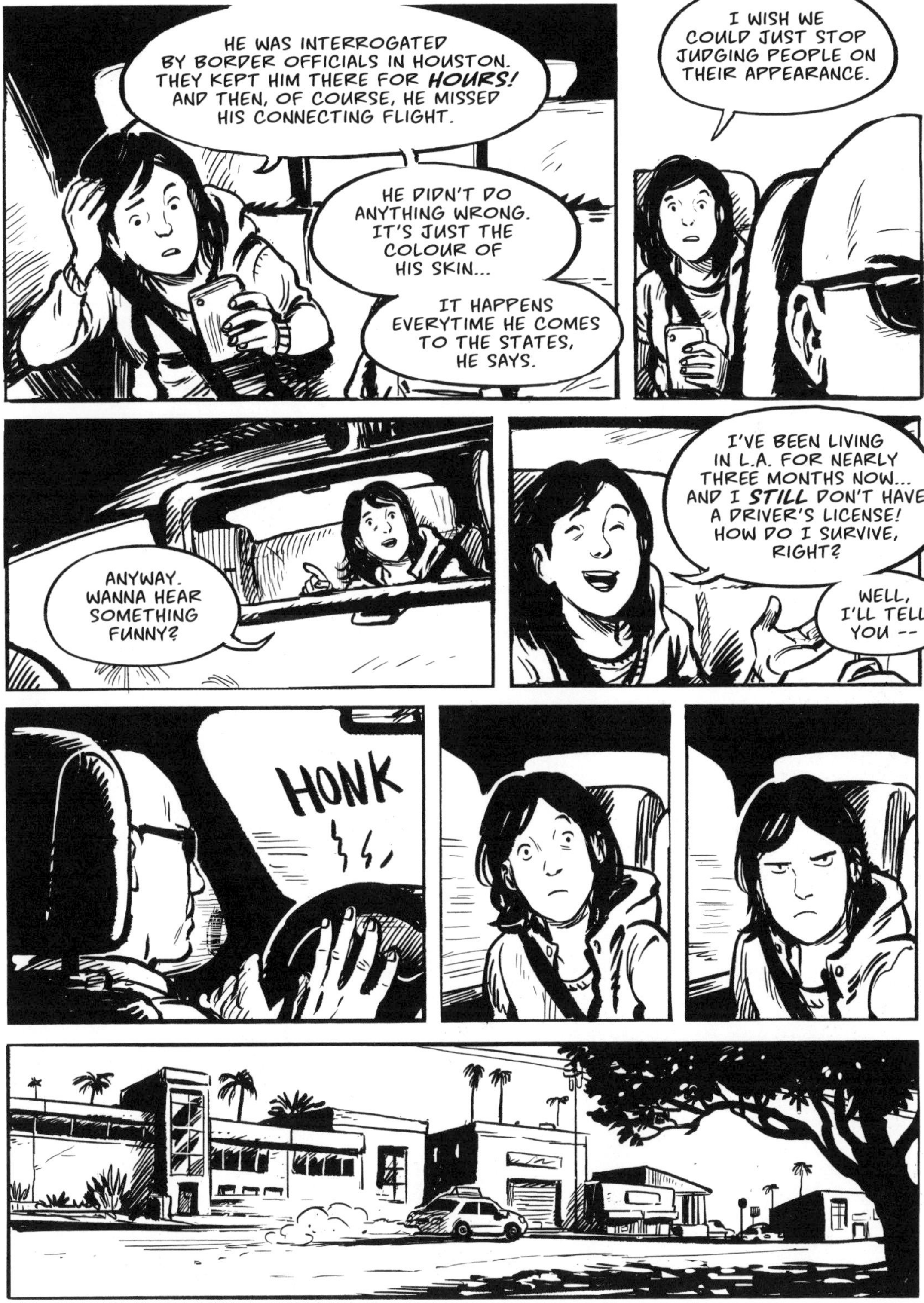
HE WAS INTERROGATED BY BORDER OFFICIALS IN HOUSTON. THEY KEPT HIM THERE FOR *HOURS!* AND THEN, OF COURSE, HE MISSED HIS CONNECTING FLIGHT.
HE DIDN'T DO ANYTHING WRONG. IT'S JUST THE COLOUR OF HIS SKIN...
IT HAPPENS EVERYTIME HE COMES TO THE STATES, HE SAYS.
I WISH WE COULD JUST STOP JUDGING PEOPLE ON THEIR APPEARANCE.
ANYWAY. WANNA HEAR SOMETHING FUNNY?
I'VE BEEN LIVING IN L.A. FOR NEARLY THREE MONTHS NOW... AND I *STILL* DON'T HAVE A DRIVER'S LICENSE! HOW DO I SURVIVE, RIGHT?
WELL, I'LL TELL YOU --
HONK

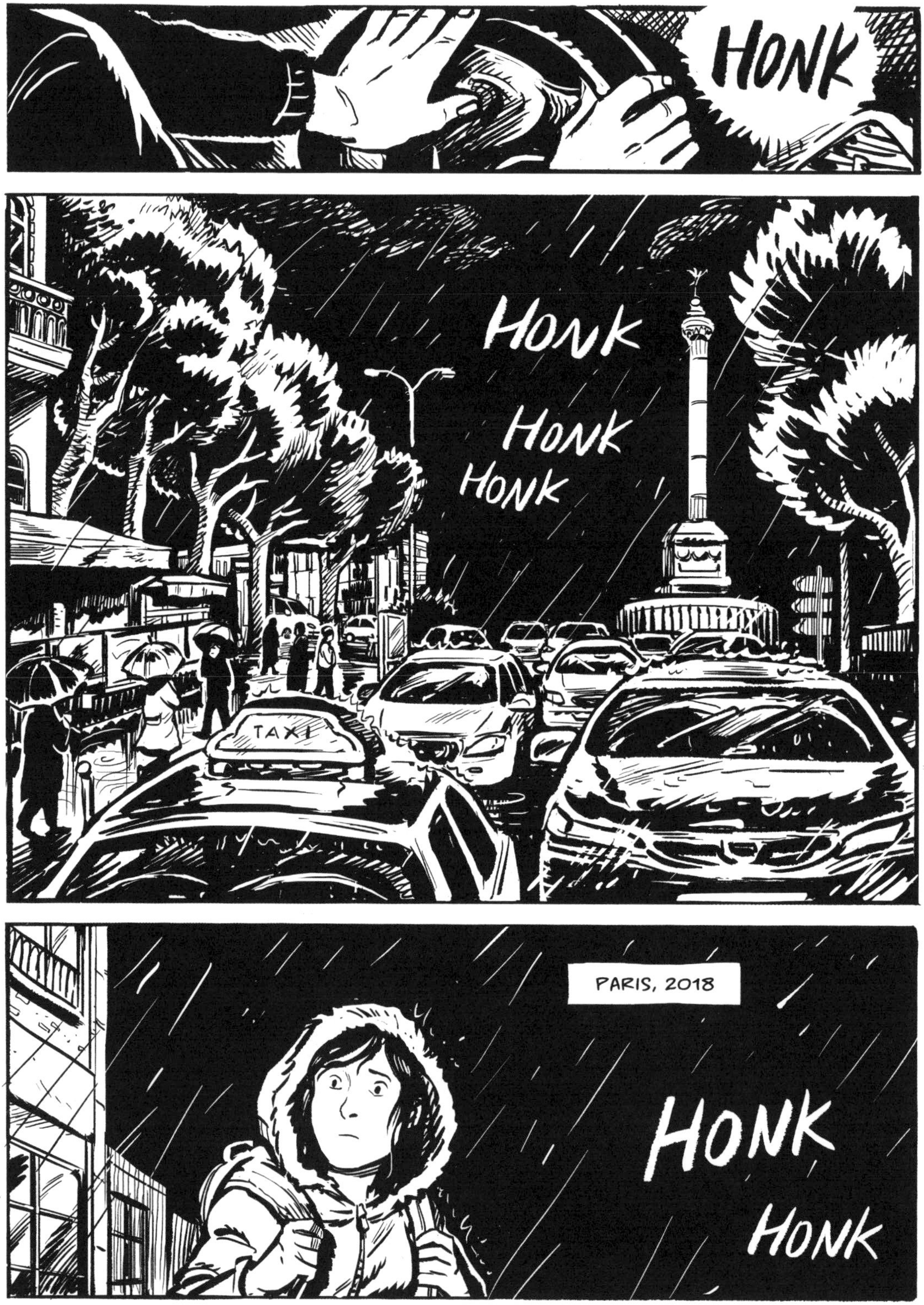
HONK
HONK
HONK
HONK
PARIS, 2018
HONK
HONK

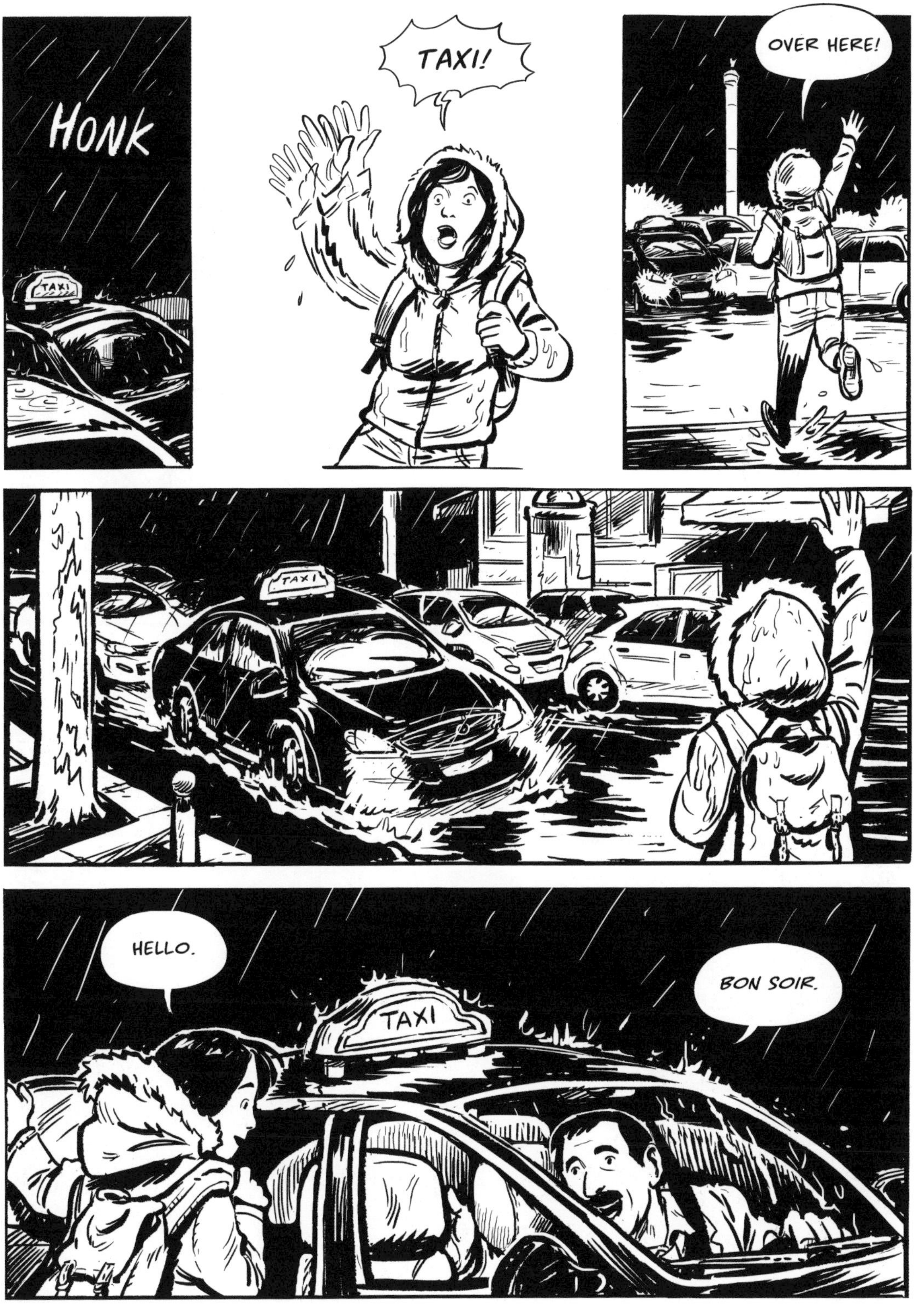
HONK
TAXI
TAXI!
OVER HERE!
TAXI
HELLO.
BON SOIR.
TAXI

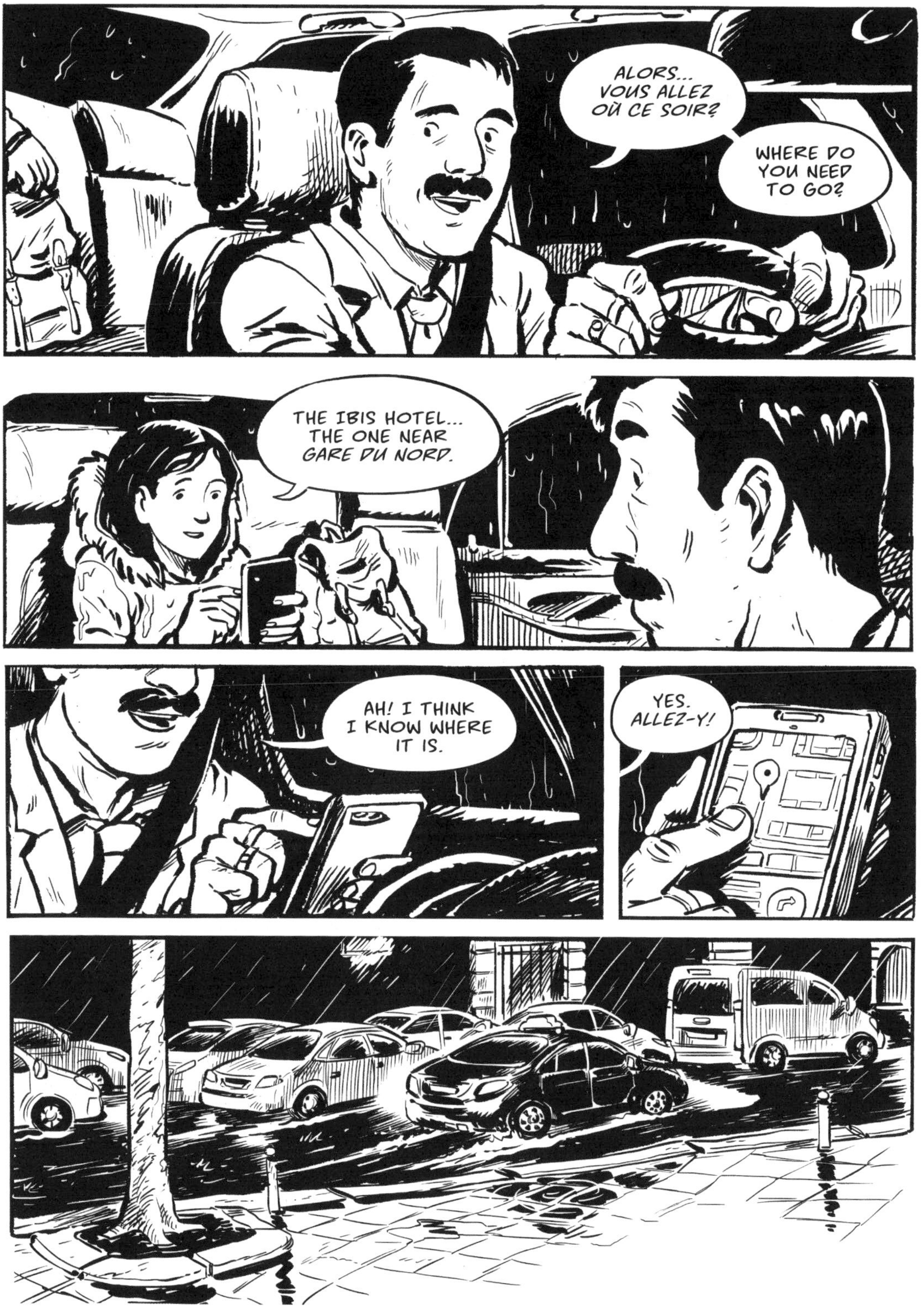
ALORS... VOUS ALLEZ OÙ CE SOIR?
WHERE DO YOU NEED TO GO?
THE IBIS HOTEL... THE ONE NEAR GARE DU NORD.
AH! I THINK I KNOW WHERE IT IS.
YES. ALLEZ-Y!

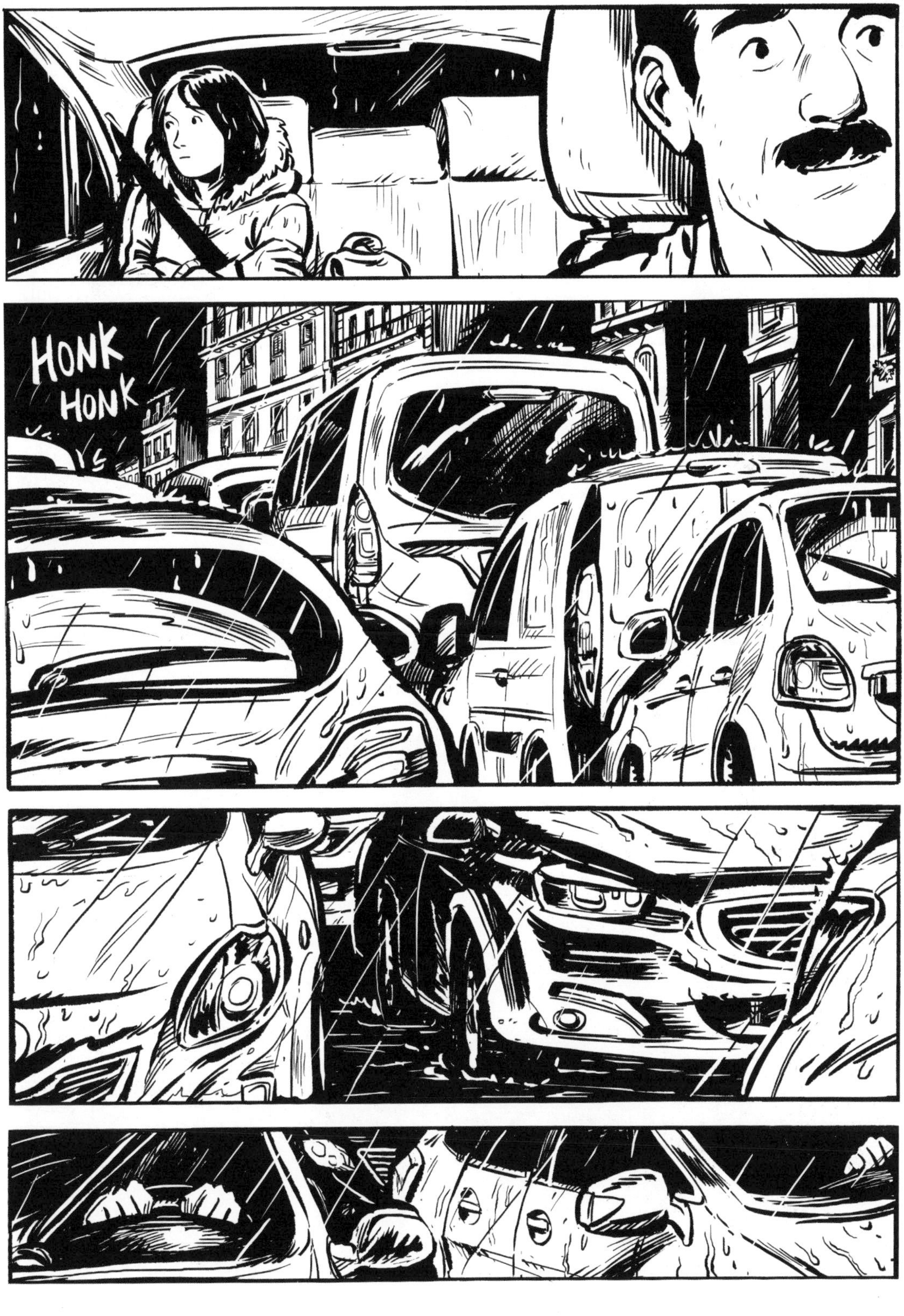
HONK
HONK

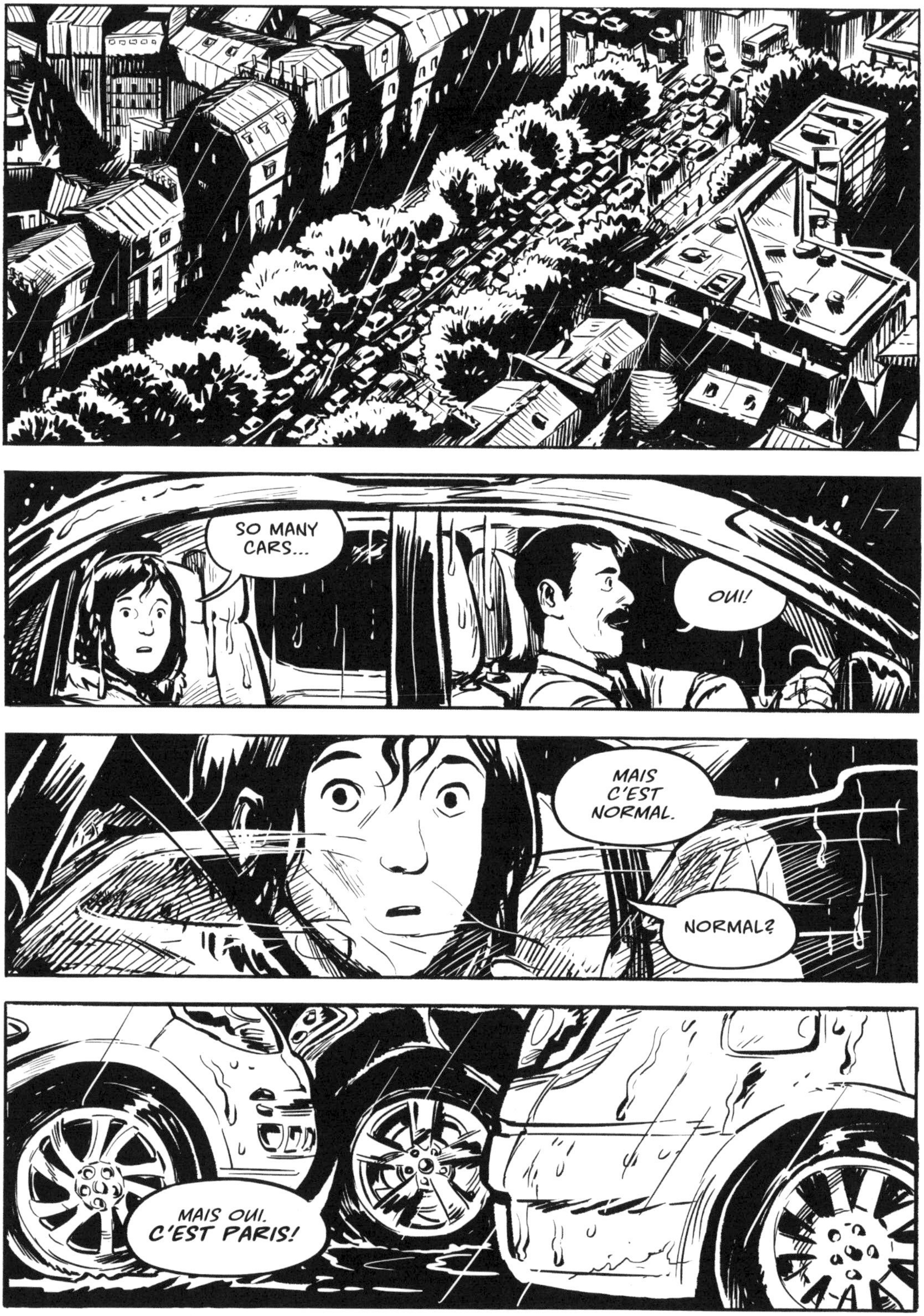
SO MANY CARS...
OUI!
MAIS C'EST NORMAL.
NORMAL?
MAIS OUI. C'EST PARIS!

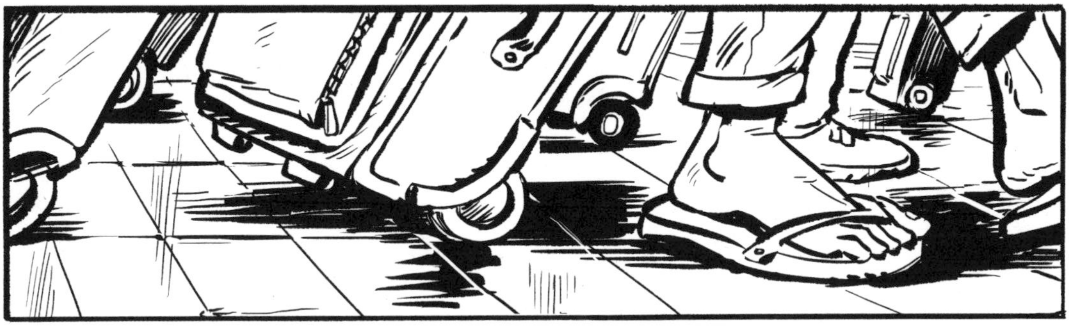

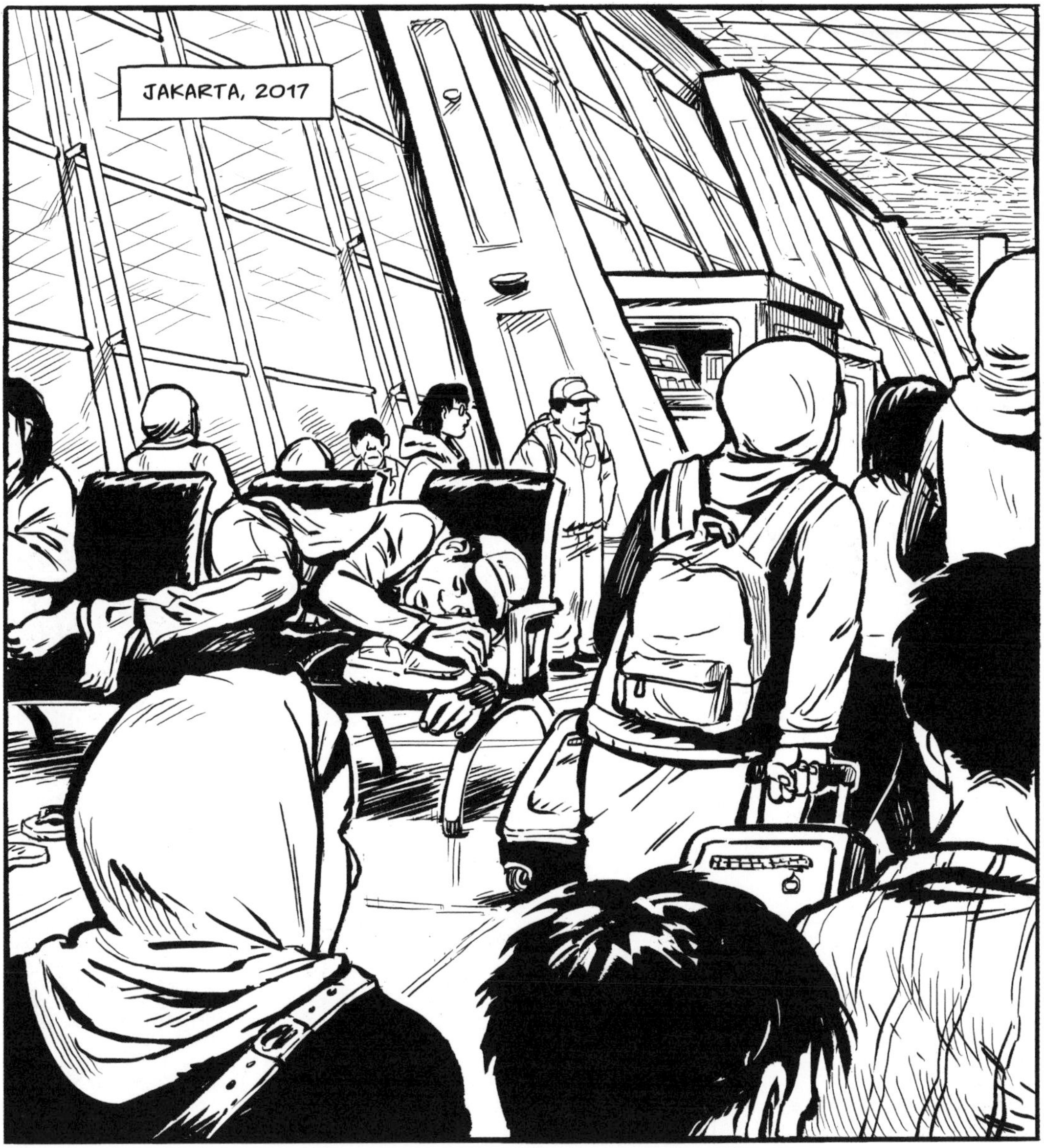
JAKARTA, 2017

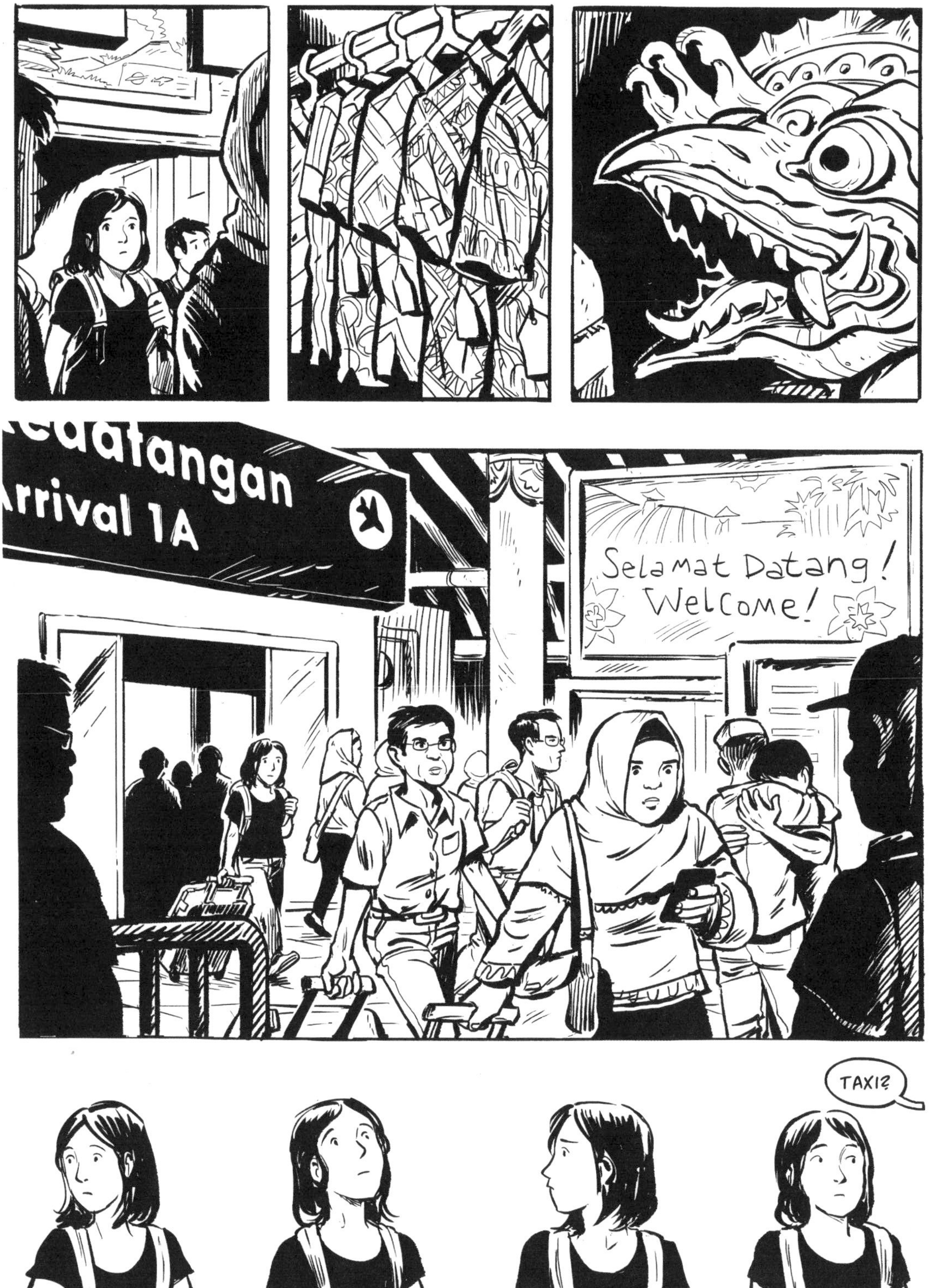
edatangan
Arrival 1A
Selamat Datang! Welcome!
TAXI?

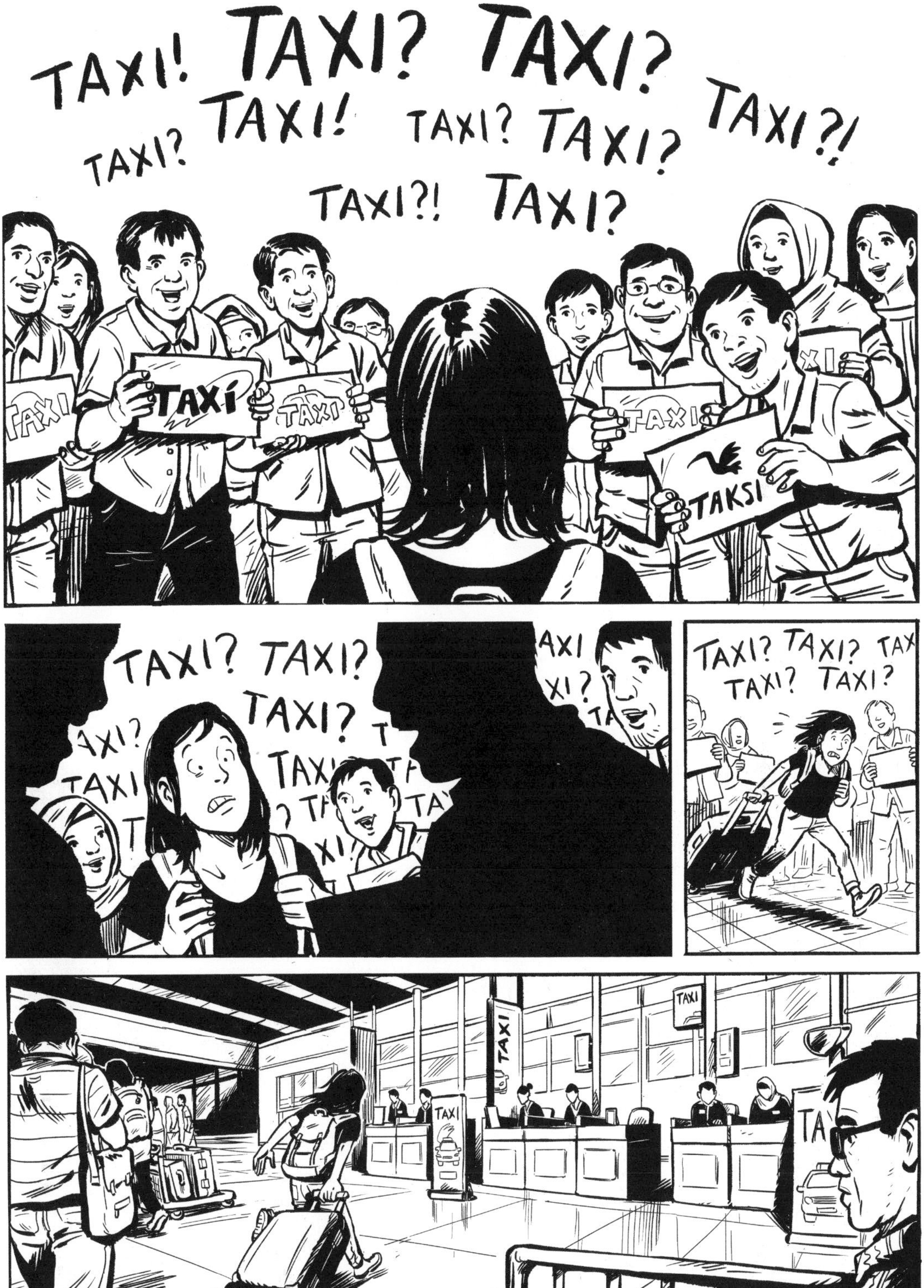
TAXI! TAXI? TAXI?
TAXI? TAXI! TAXI? TAXI? TAXI?!
TAXI?! TAXI?
TAXI
TAXI
TAXI
TAXI
TAKSI
TAXI? TAXI?
TAXI?
TAXI?
TAXI
TAXI? TAXI?
TAXI? TAXI?
TAXI
TAXI
TAXI

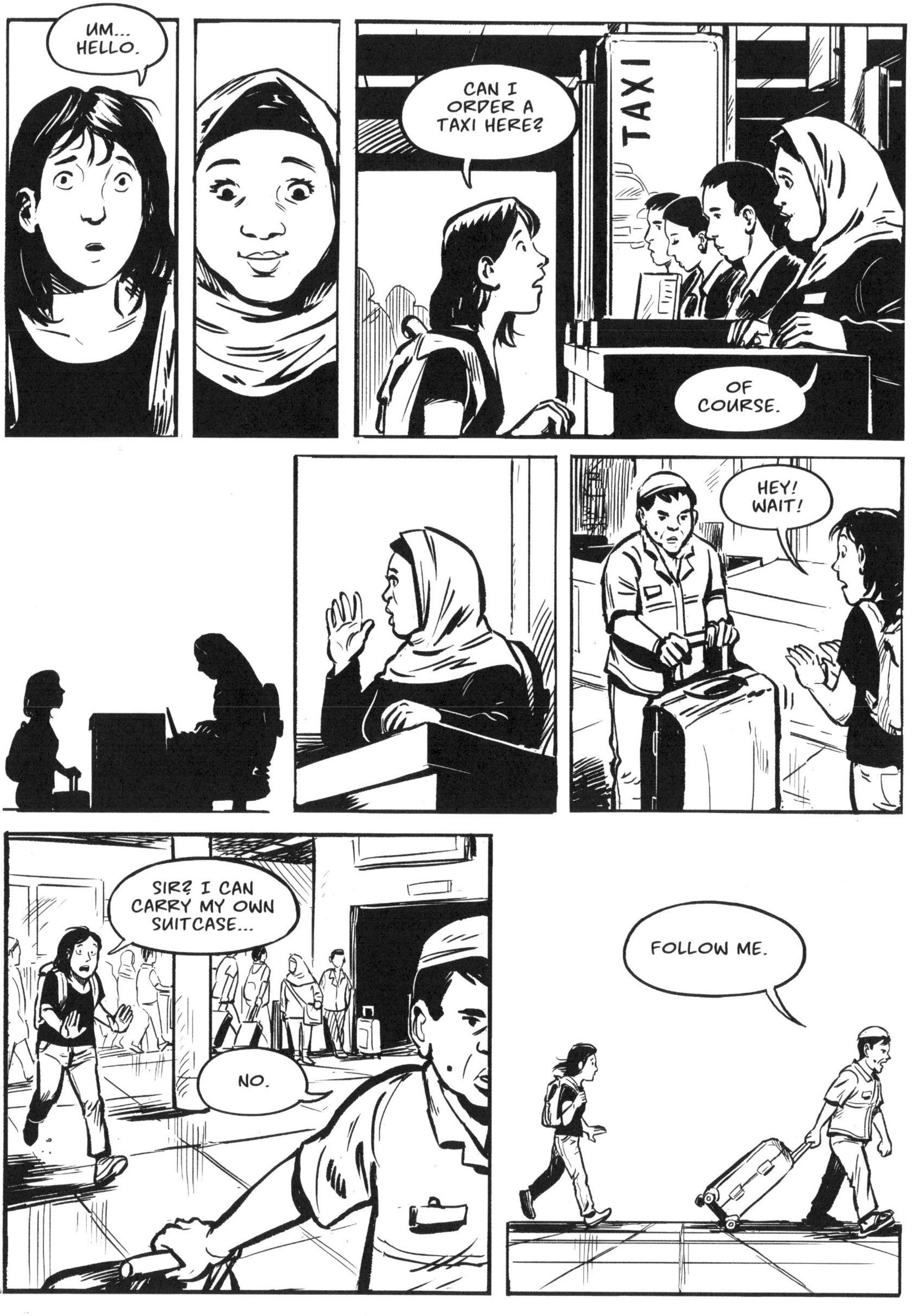
UM... HELLO.
CAN I ORDER A TAXI HERE?
TAXI
OF COURSE.
HEY! WAIT!
SIR? I CAN CARRY MY OWN SUITCASE...
NO.
FOLLOW ME.

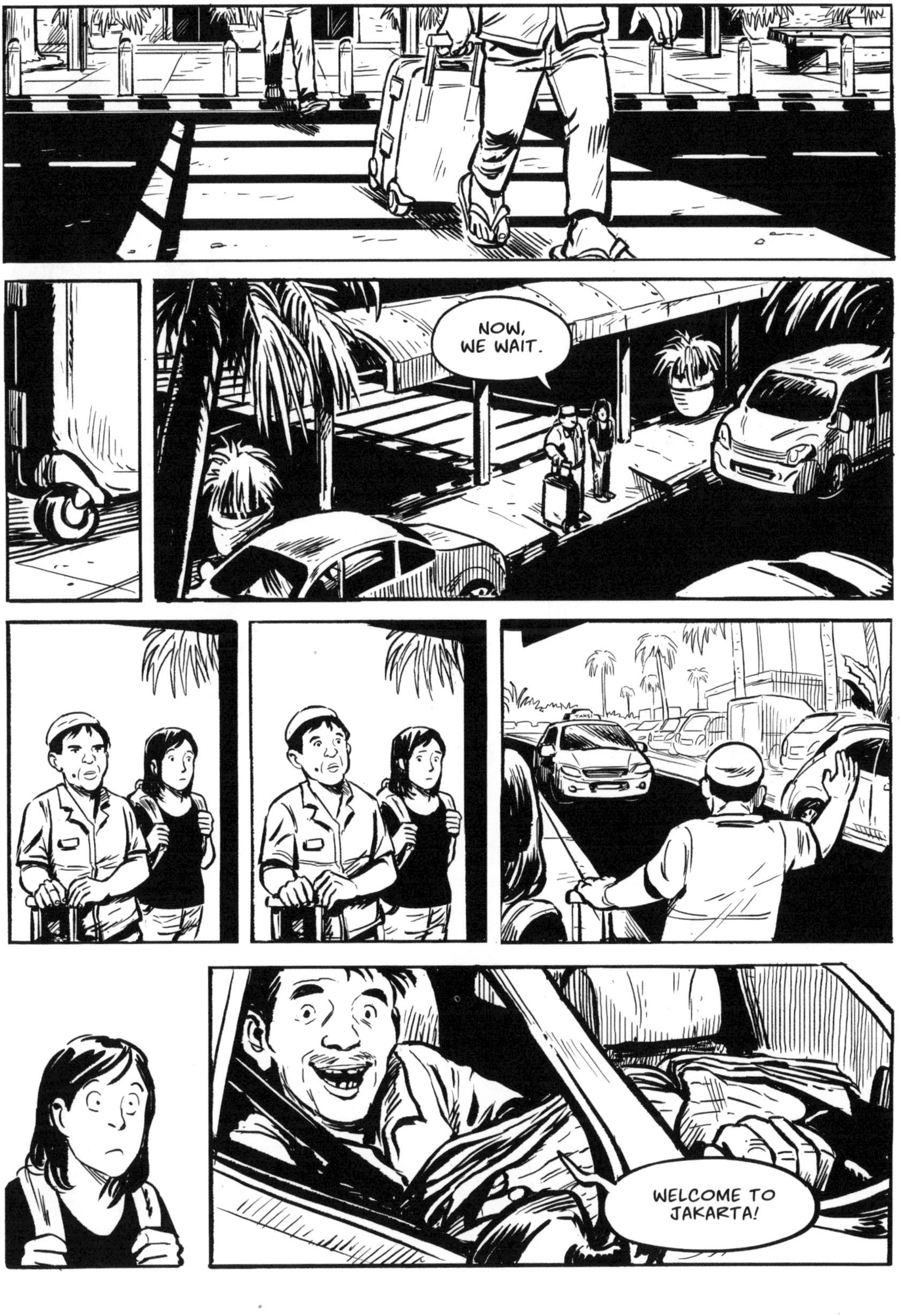
NOW, WE WAIT.
WELCOME TO JAKARTA!

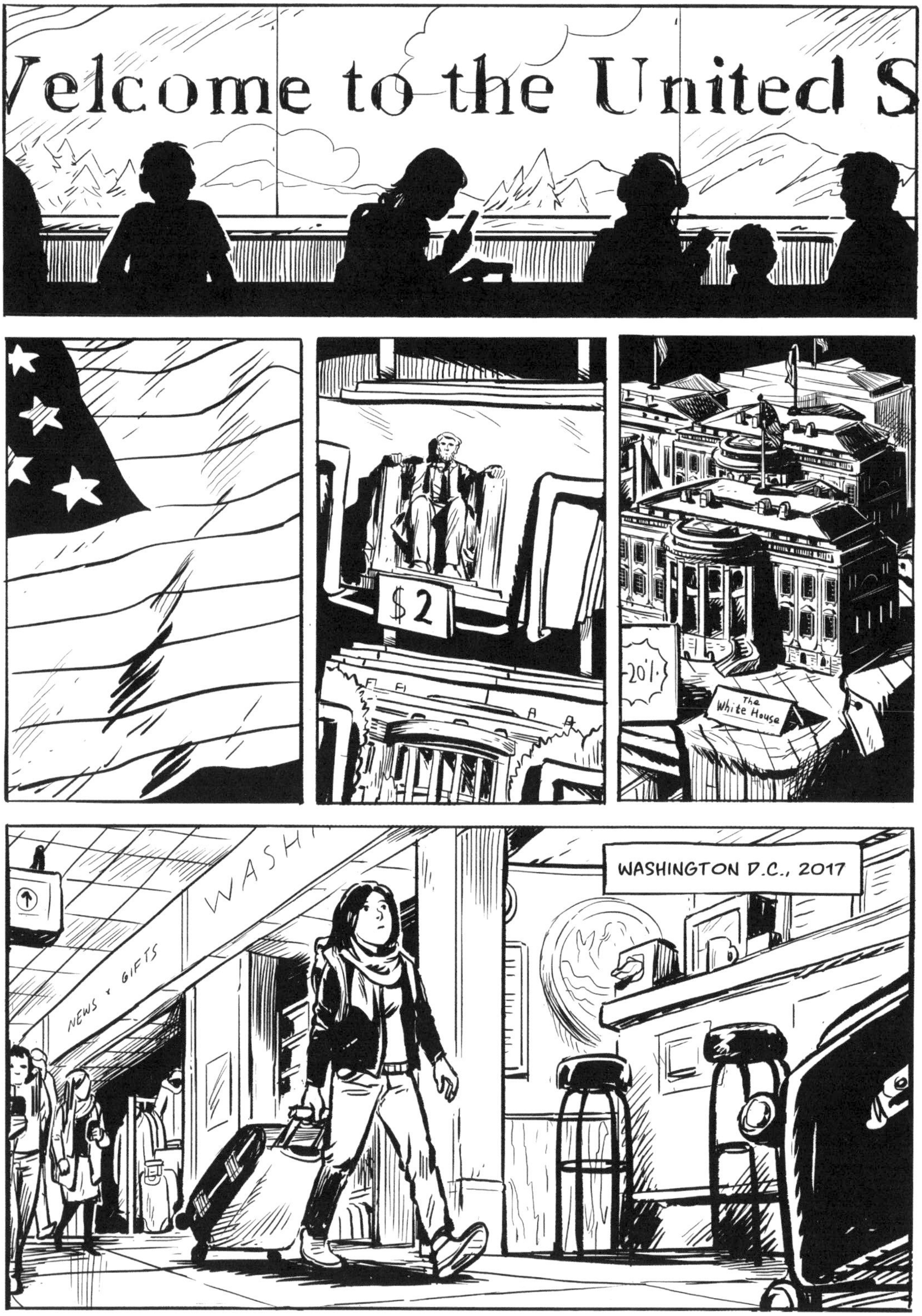
elcome to the United
$2
The White House
NEWS + GIFTS
WASH
WASHINGTON D.C., 2017

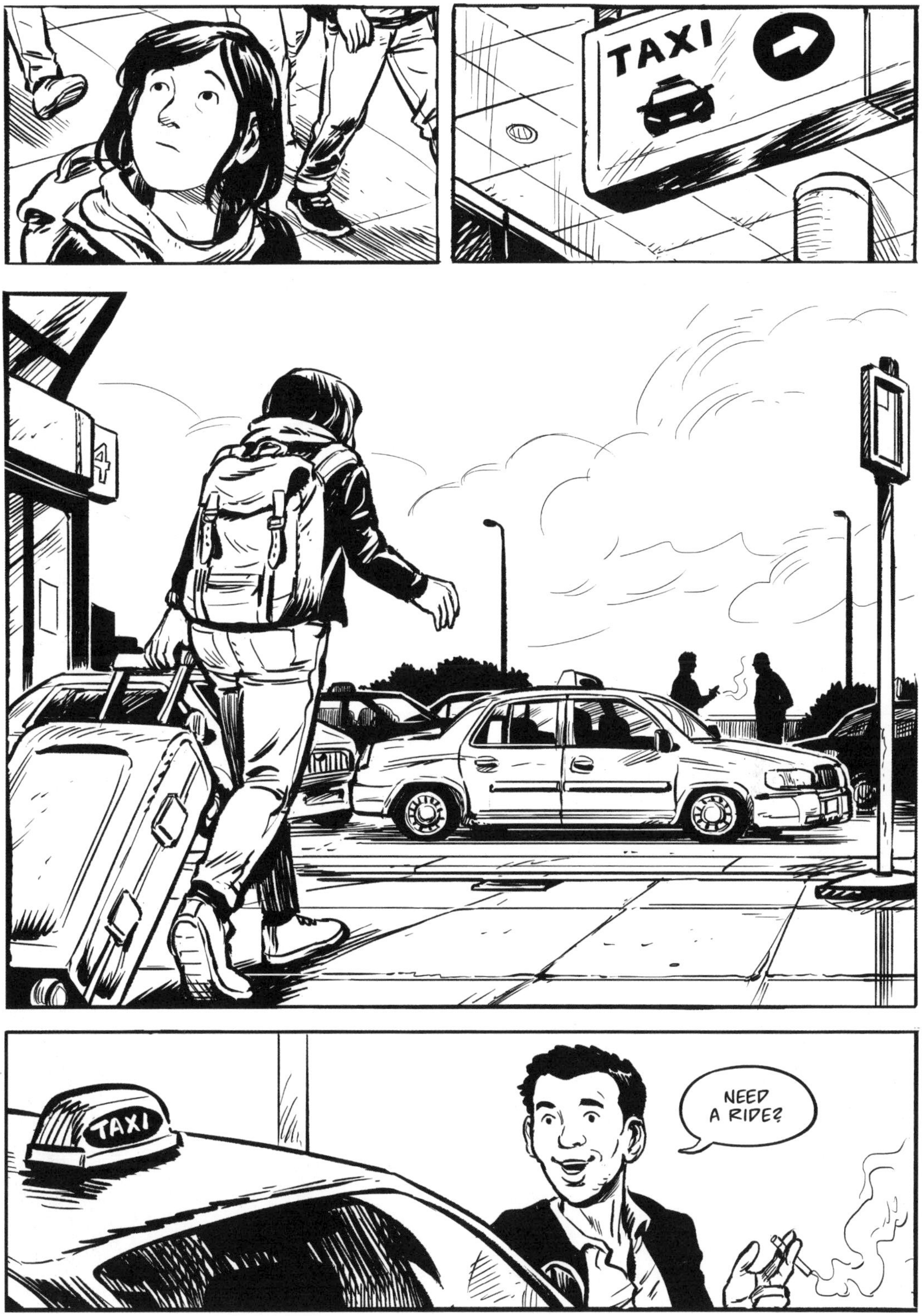
TAXI
4
TAXI
NEED A RIDE?

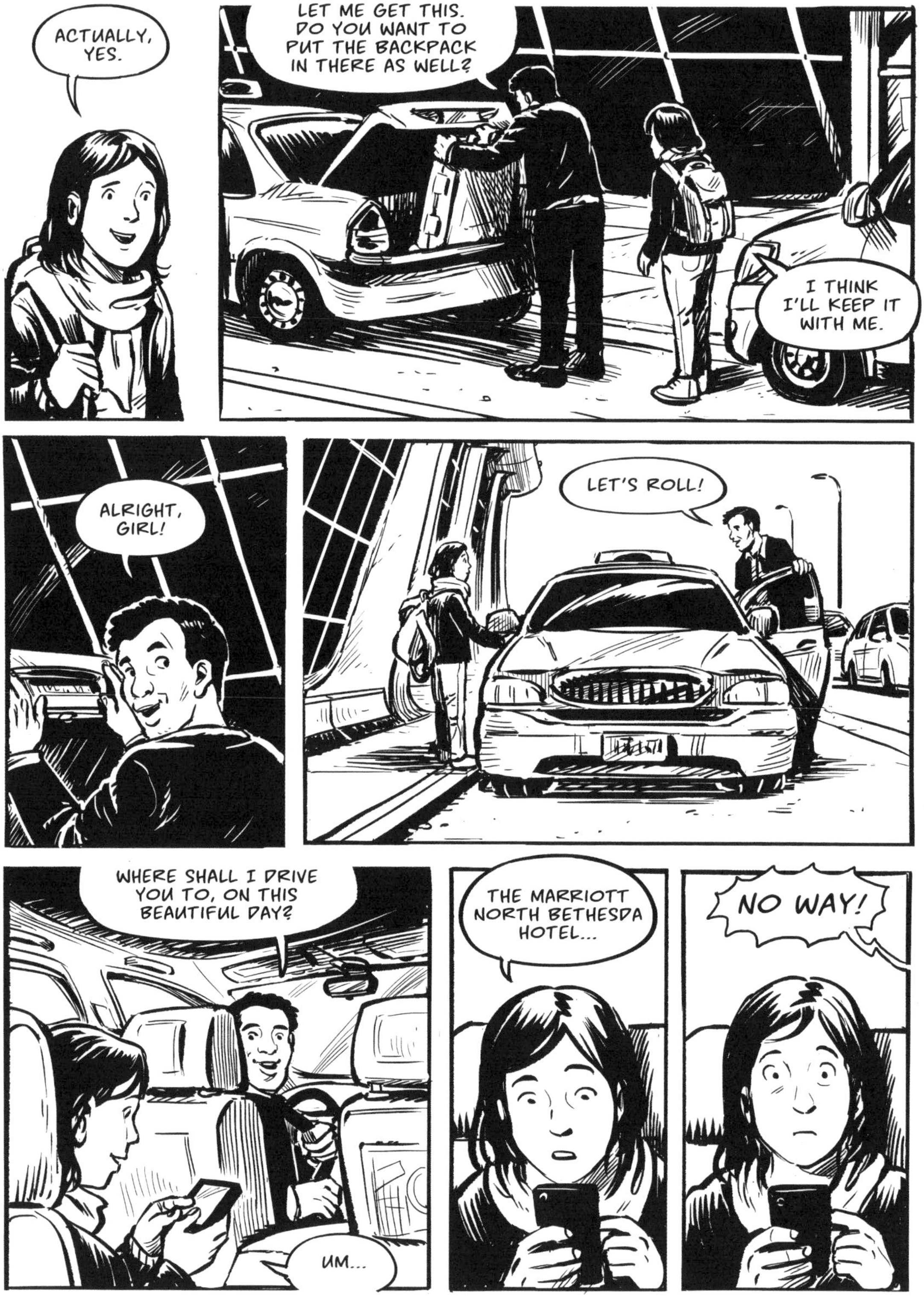
ACTUALLY, YES.
LET ME GET THIS. DO YOU WANT TO PUT THE BACKPACK IN THERE AS WELL?
I THINK I'LL KEEP IT WITH ME.
ALRIGHT, GIRL!
LET'S ROLL!
WHERE SHALL I DRIVE YOU TO, ON THIS BEAUTIFUL DAY?
UM...
THE MARRIOTT NORTH BETHESDA HOTEL...
NO WAY!

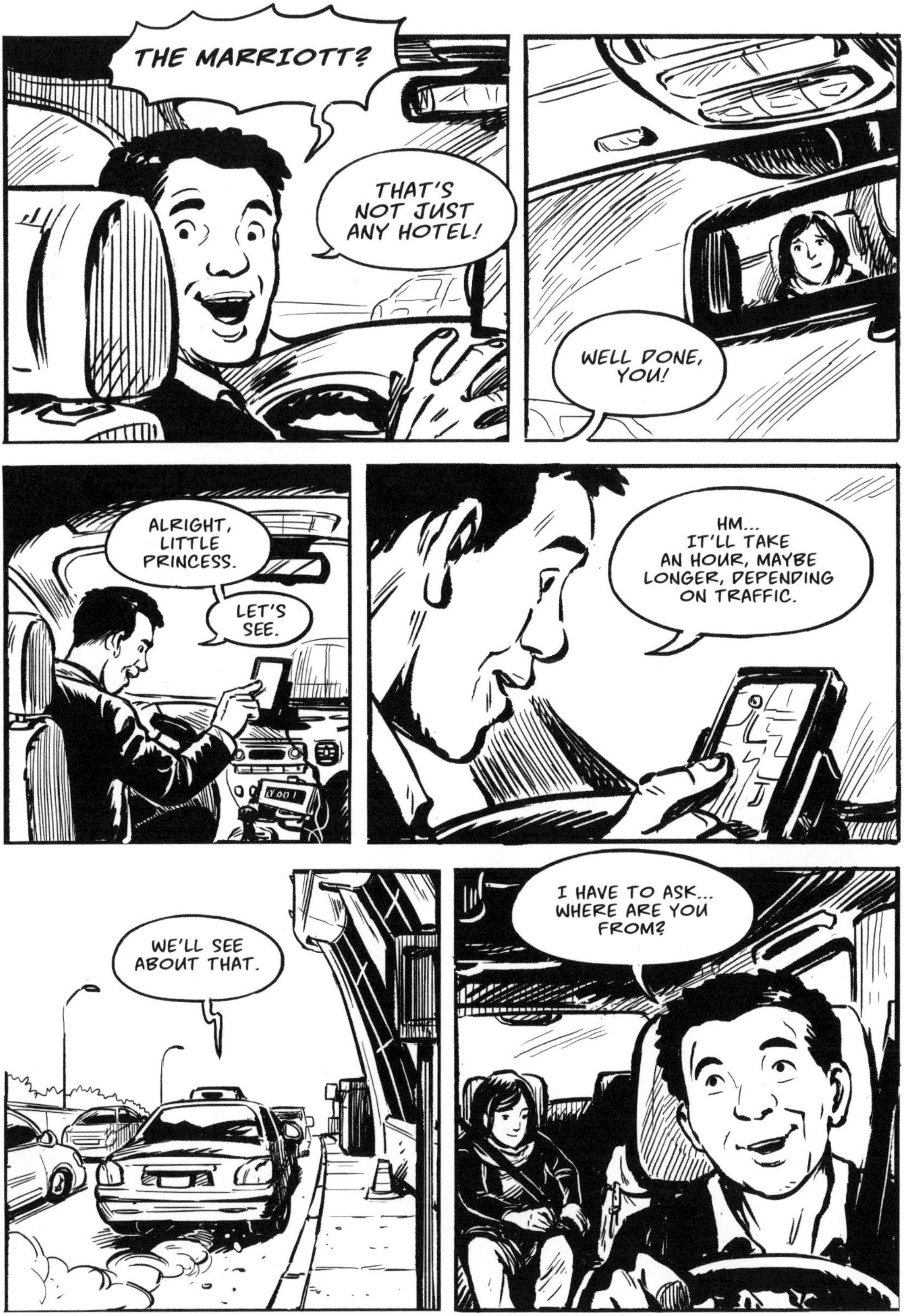
THE MARRIOTT?
THAT'S NOT JUST ANY HOTEL!
WELL DONE, YOU!
ALRIGHT, LITTLE PRINCESS.
LET'S SEE.
HM... IT'LL TAKE AN HOUR, MAYBE LONGER, DEPENDING ON TRAFFIC.
WE'LL SEE ABOUT THAT.
I HAVE TO ASK... WHERE ARE YOU FROM?

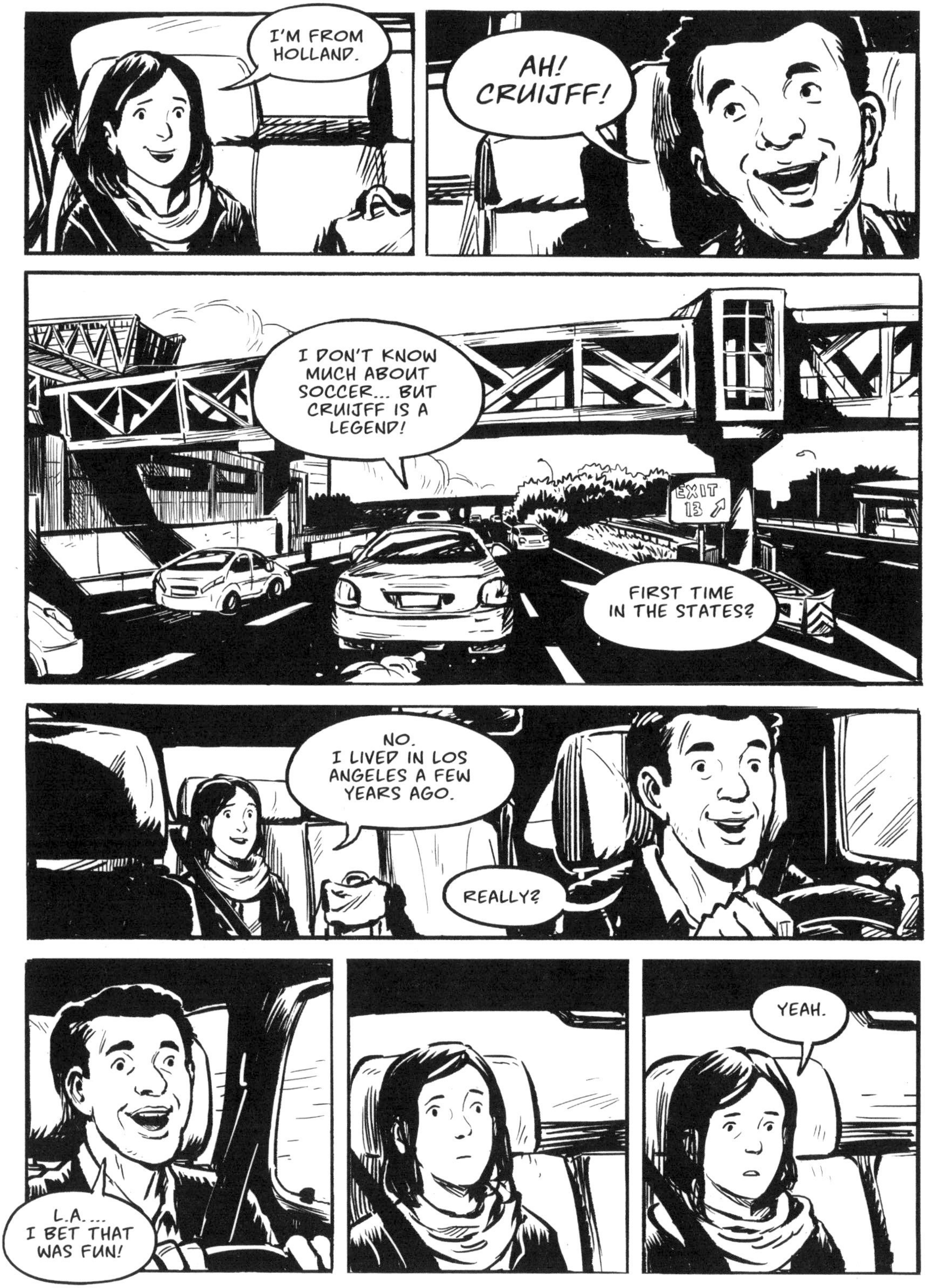
I'M FROM HOLLAND.
AH! CRUIJFF!
I DON'T KNOW MUCH ABOUT SOCCER... BUT CRUIJFF IS A LEGEND!
EXIT 13
FIRST TIME IN THE STATES?
NO. I LIVED IN LOS ANGELES A FEW YEARS AGO.
REALLY?
L.A.... I BET THAT WAS FUN!
YEAH.

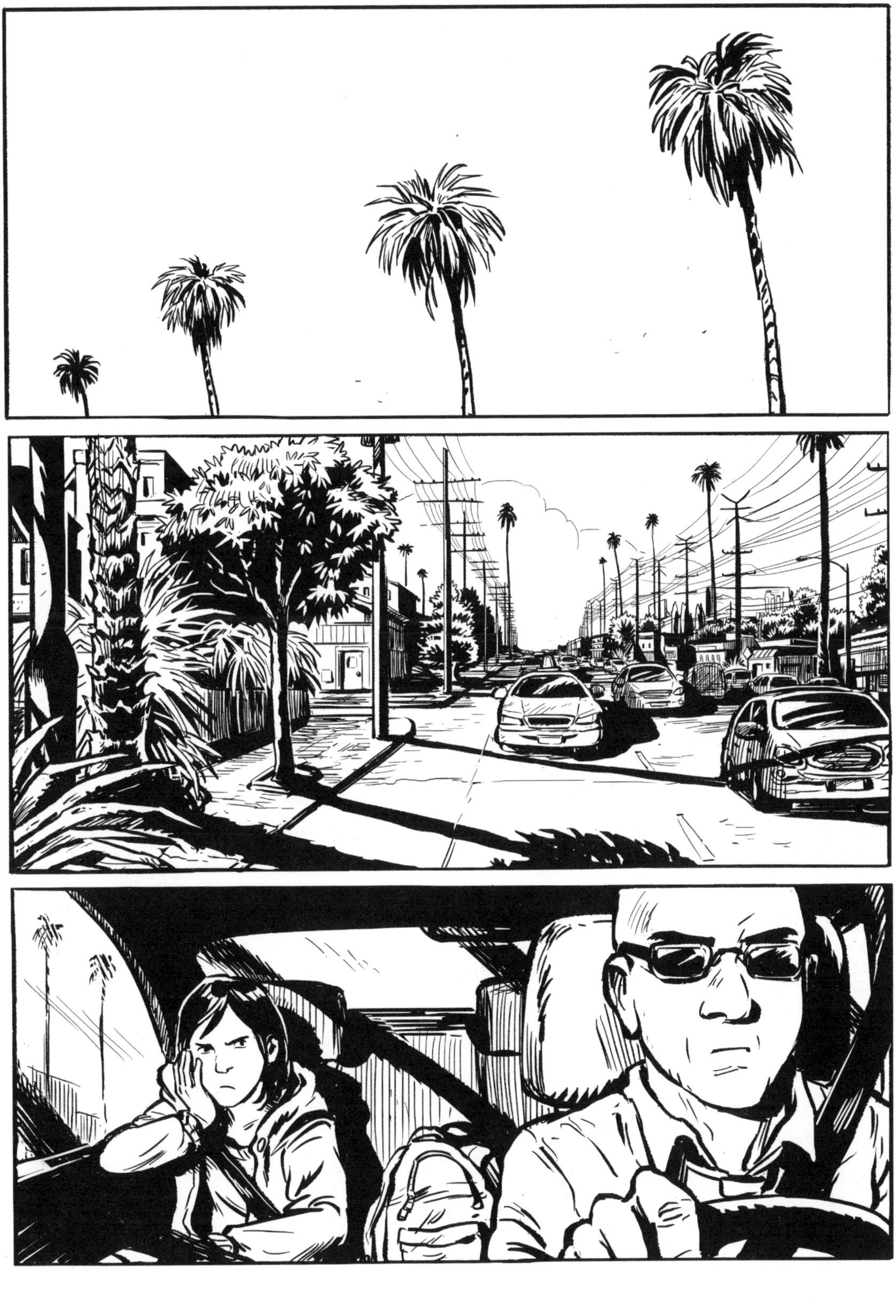

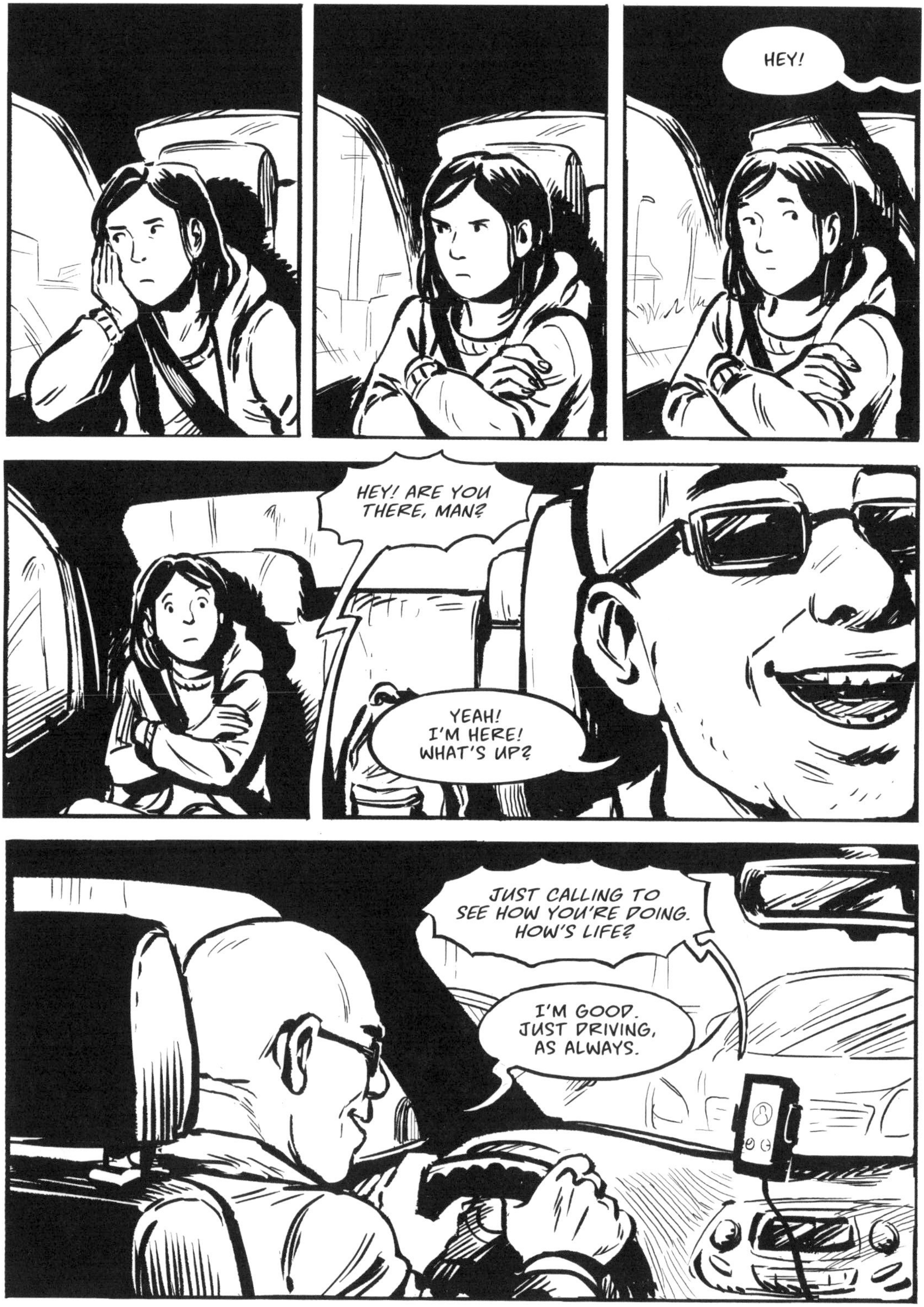
HEY!
HEY! ARE YOU THERE, MAN?
YEAH! I'M HERE! WHAT'S UP?
JUST CALLING TO SEE HOW YOU'RE DOING. HOW'S LIFE?
I'M GOOD. JUST DRIVING, AS ALWAYS.

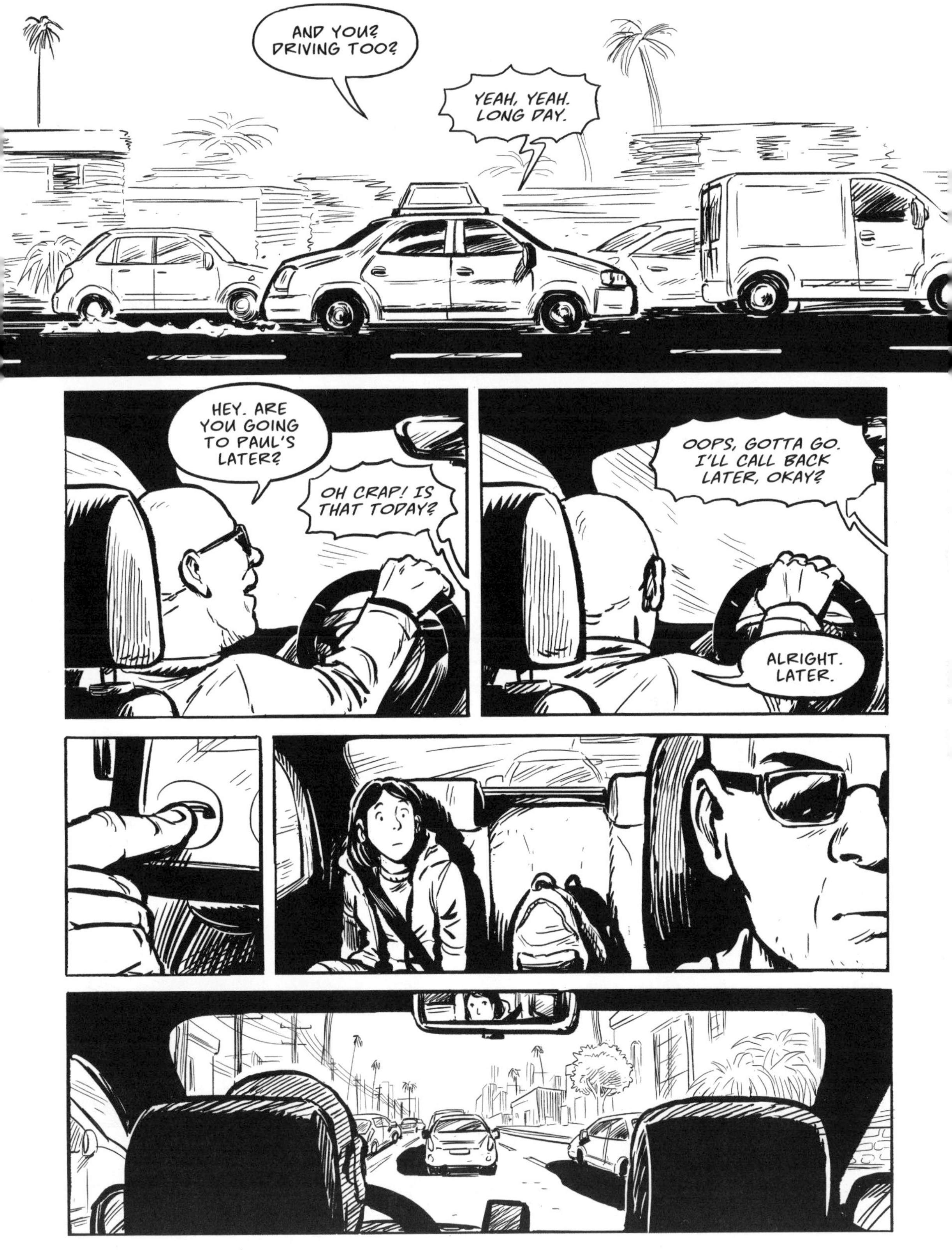
AND YOU? DRIVING TOO?
YEAH, YEAH. LONG DAY.
HEY. ARE YOU GOING TO PAUL'S LATER?
OH CRAP! IS THAT TODAY?
OOPS, GOTTA GO. I'LL CALL BACK LATER, OKAY?
ALRIGHT. LATER.

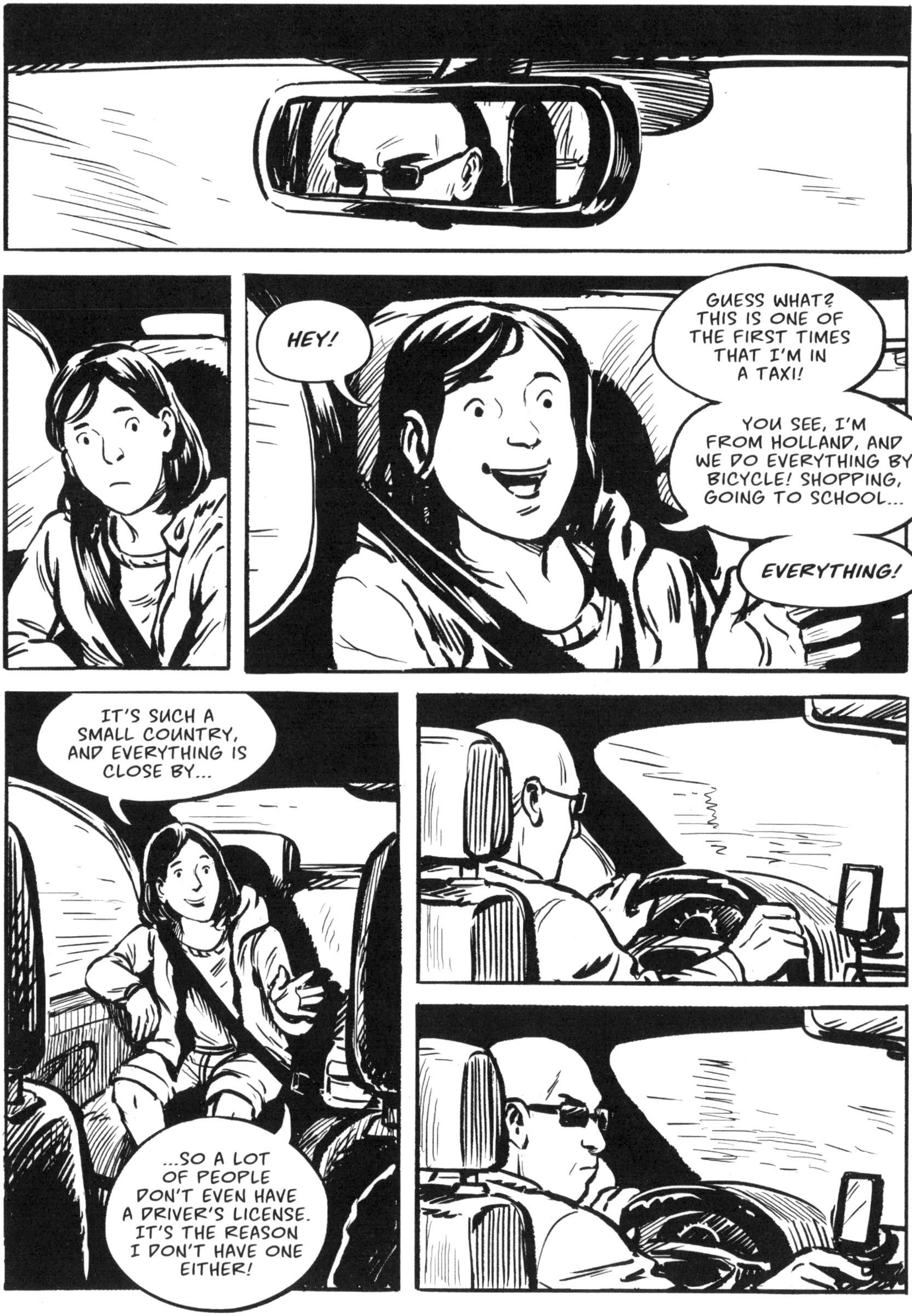
HEY!
GUESS WHAT? THIS IS ONE OF THE FIRST TIMES THAT I'M IN A TAXI!
YOU SEE, I'M FROM HOLLAND, AND WE DO EVERYTHING BY BICYCLE! SHOPPING, GOING TO SCHOOL...
EVERYTHING!
IT'S SUCH A SMALL COUNTRY, AND EVERYTHING IS CLOSE BY...
...SO A LOT OF PEOPLE DON'T EVEN HAVE A DRIVER'S LICENSE. IT'S THE REASON I DON'T HAVE ONE EITHER!

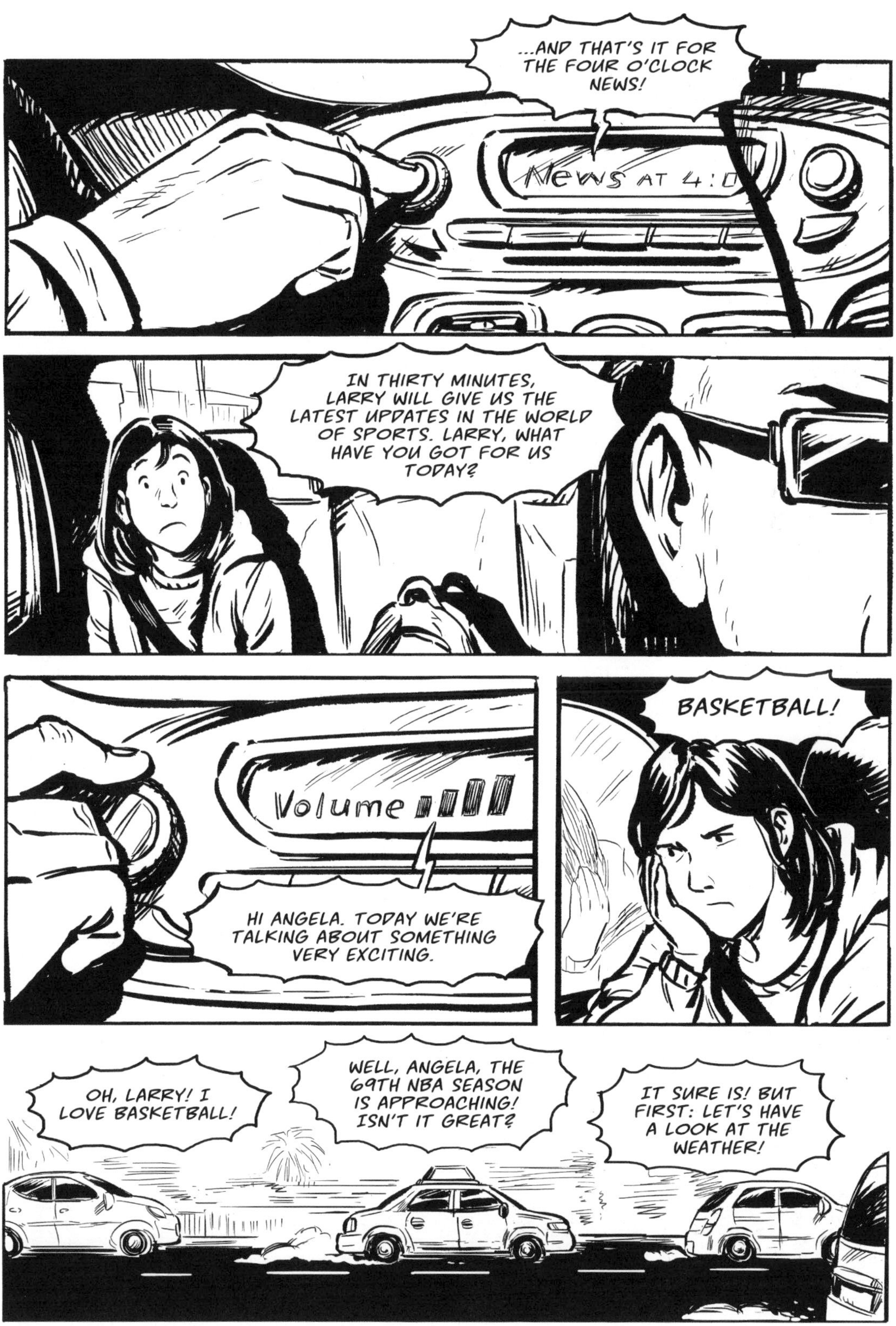
...AND THAT'S IT FOR THE FOUR O'CLOCK NEWS!
News AT 4:0
IN THIRTY MINUTES, LARRY WILL GIVE US THE LATEST UPDATES IN THE WORLD OF SPORTS. LARRY, WHAT HAVE YOU GOT FOR US TODAY?
Volume
HI ANGELA. TODAY WE'RE TALKING ABOUT SOMETHING VERY EXCITING.
BASKETBALL!
OH, LARRY! I LOVE BASKETBALL!
WELL, ANGELA, THE 69TH NBA SEASON IS APPROACHING! ISN'T IT GREAT?
IT SURE IS! BUT FIRST: LET'S HAVE A LOOK AT THE WEATHER!

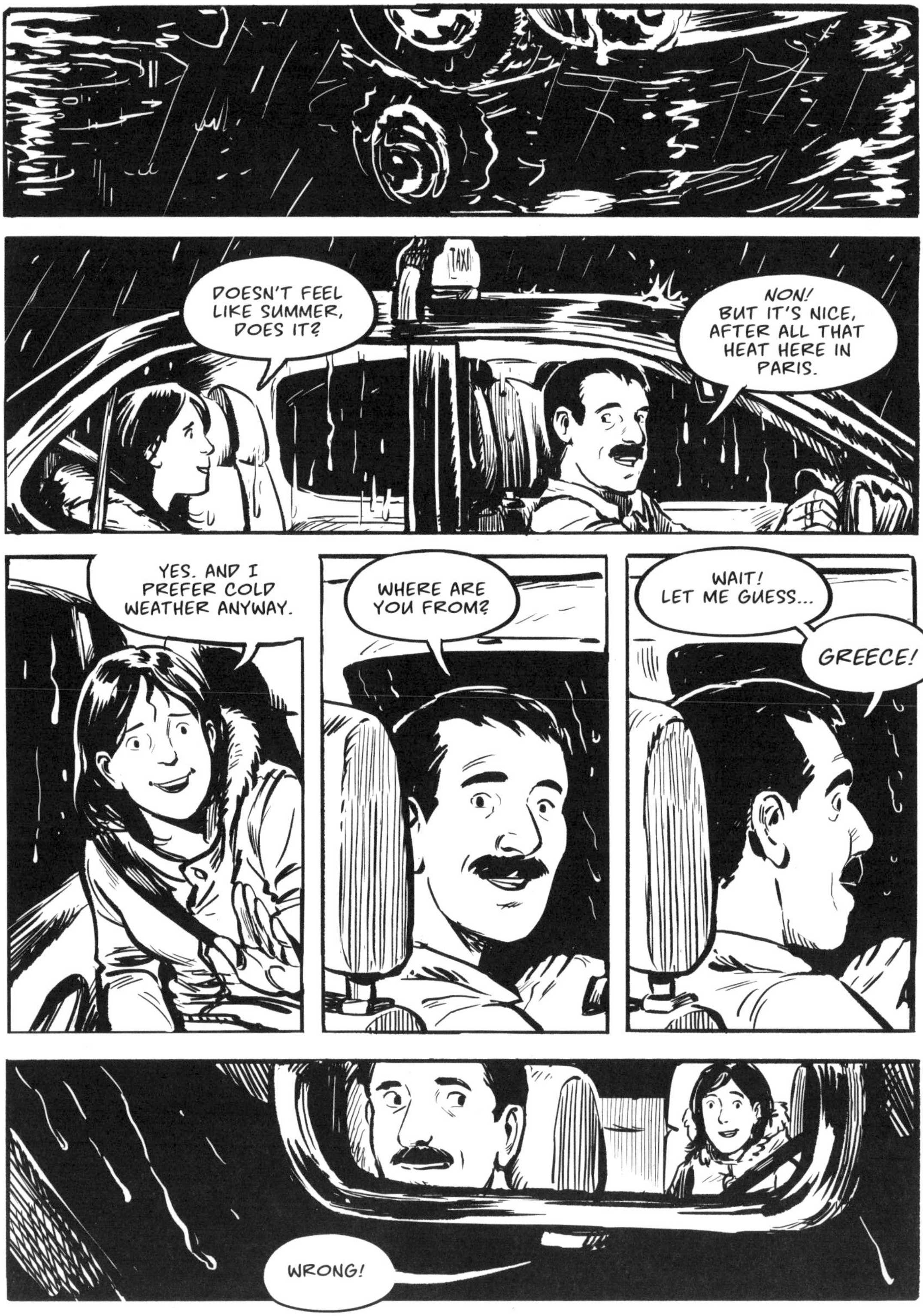
DOESN'T FEEL LIKE SUMMER, DOES IT?
NON! BUT IT'S NICE, AFTER ALL THAT HEAT HERE IN PARIS.
YES. AND I PREFER COLD WEATHER ANYWAY.
WHERE ARE YOU FROM?
WAIT! LET ME GUESS...
GREECE!
WRONG!

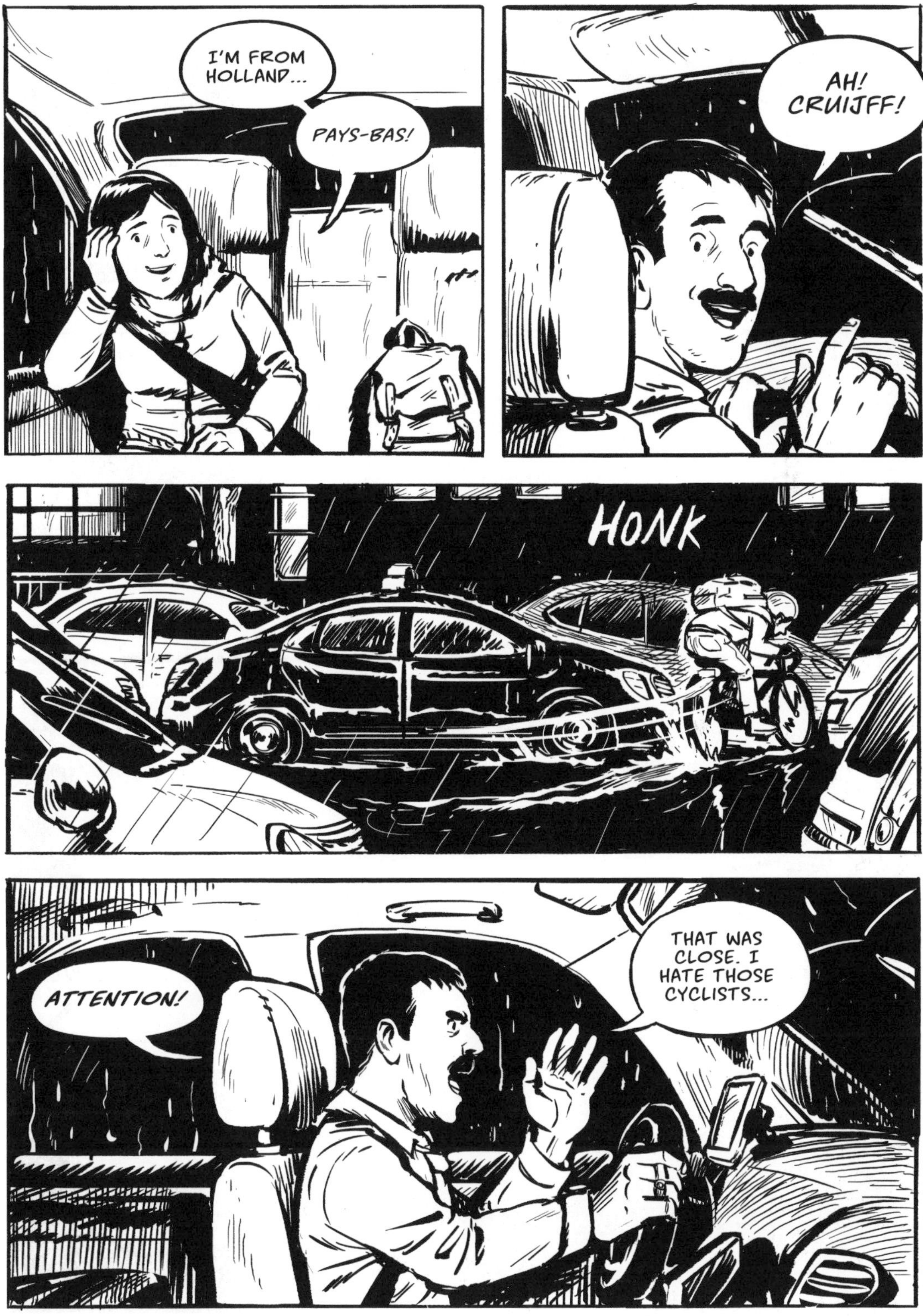
I'M FROM HOLLAND...
PAYS-BAS!
AH! CRUIJFF!
HONK
ATTENTION!
THAT WAS CLOSE. I HATE THOSE CYCLISTS...

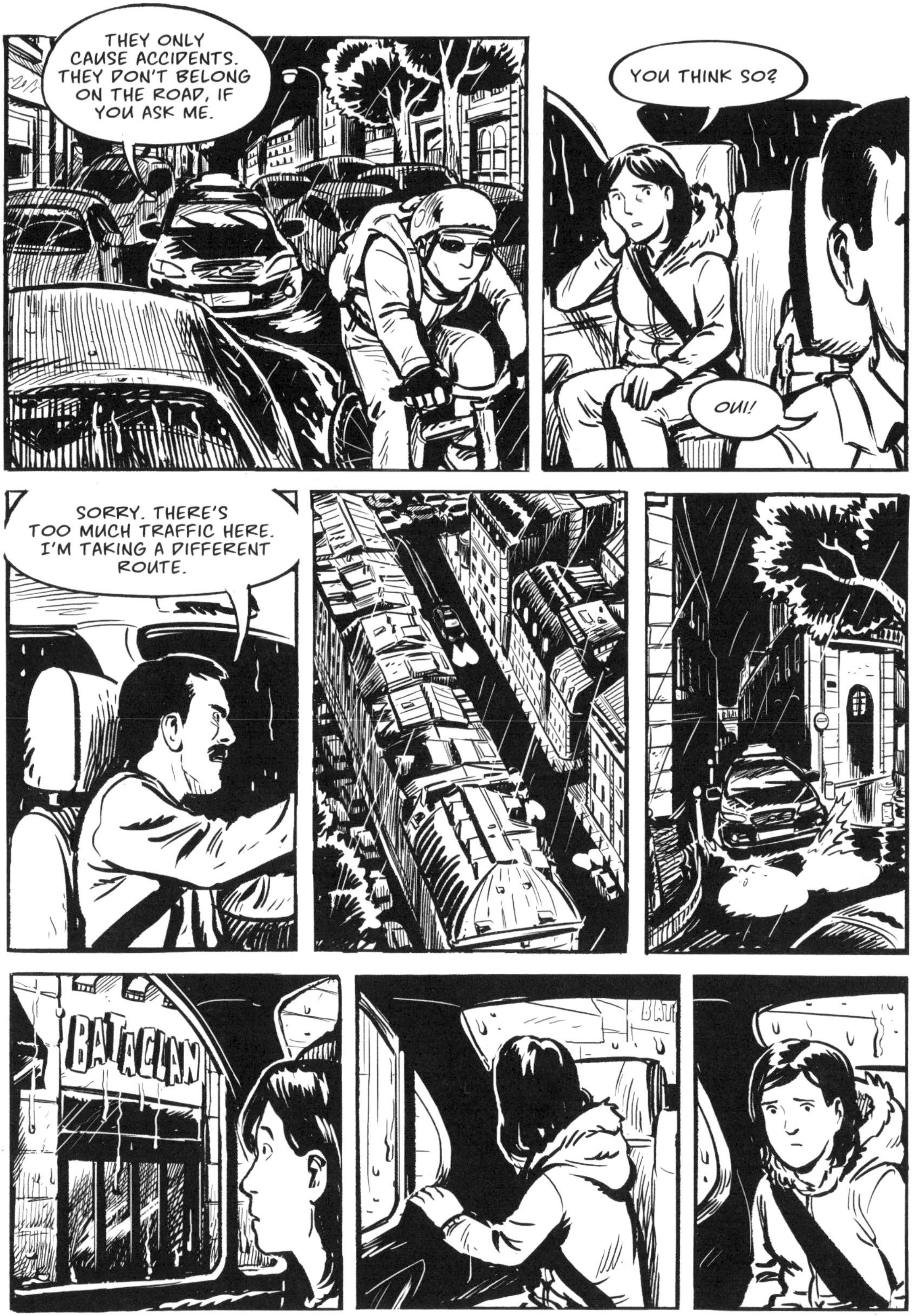
THEY ONLY CAUSE ACCIDENTS. THEY DON'T BELONG ON THE ROAD, IF YOU ASK ME.
YOU THINK SO?
OUI!
SORRY. THERE'S TOO MUCH TRAFFIC HERE. I'M TAKING A DIFFERENT ROUTE.
BATACLAN
BAT

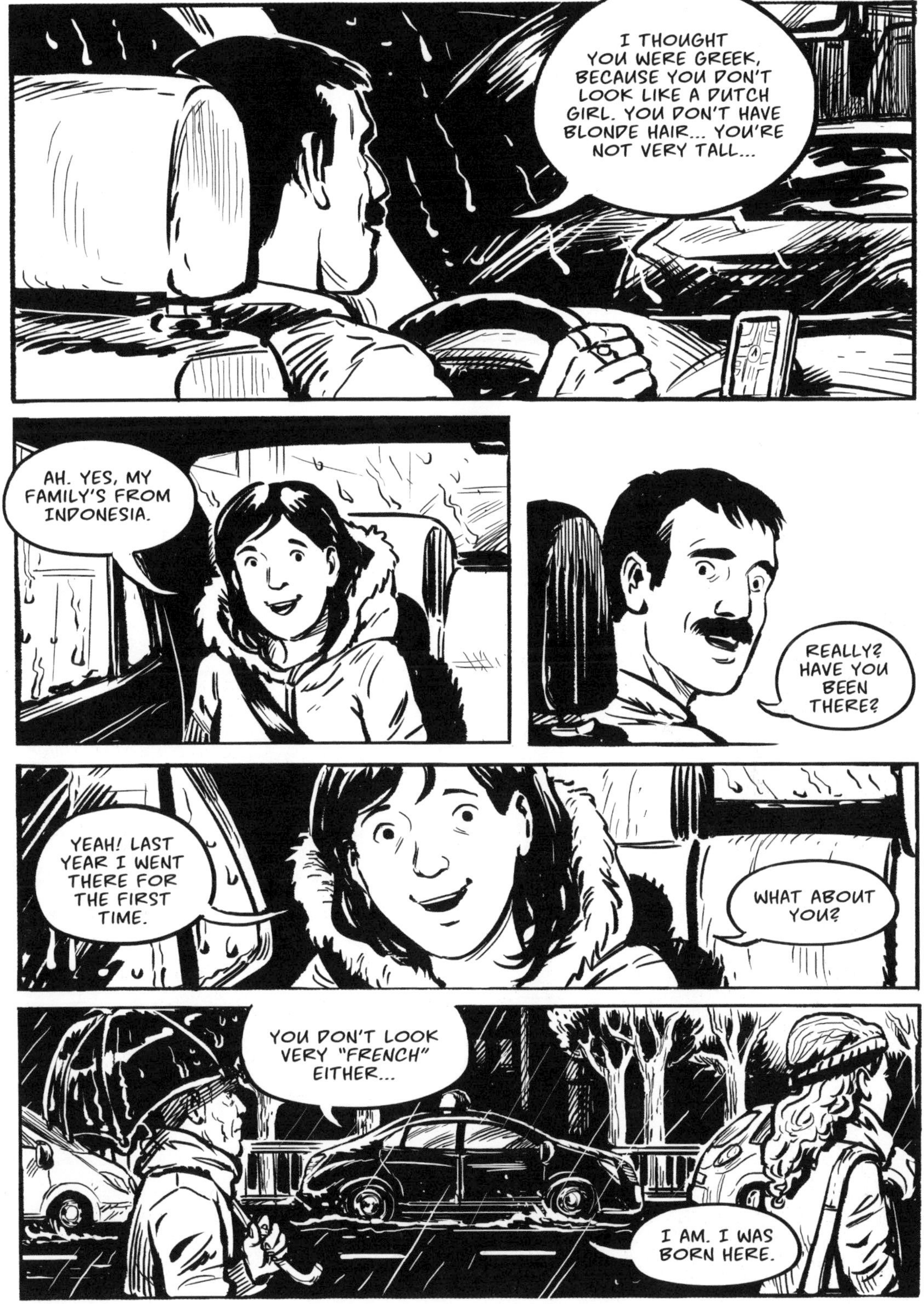
I THOUGHT YOU WERE GREEK, BECAUSE YOU DON'T LOOK LIKE A DUTCH GIRL. YOU DON'T HAVE BLONDE HAIR... YOU'RE NOT VERY TALL...
AH. YES, MY FAMILY'S FROM INDONESIA.
REALLY? HAVE YOU BEEN THERE?
YEAH! LAST YEAR I WENT THERE FOR THE FIRST TIME.
WHAT ABOUT YOU?
YOU DON'T LOOK VERY "FRENCH" EITHER...
I AM. I WAS BORN HERE.

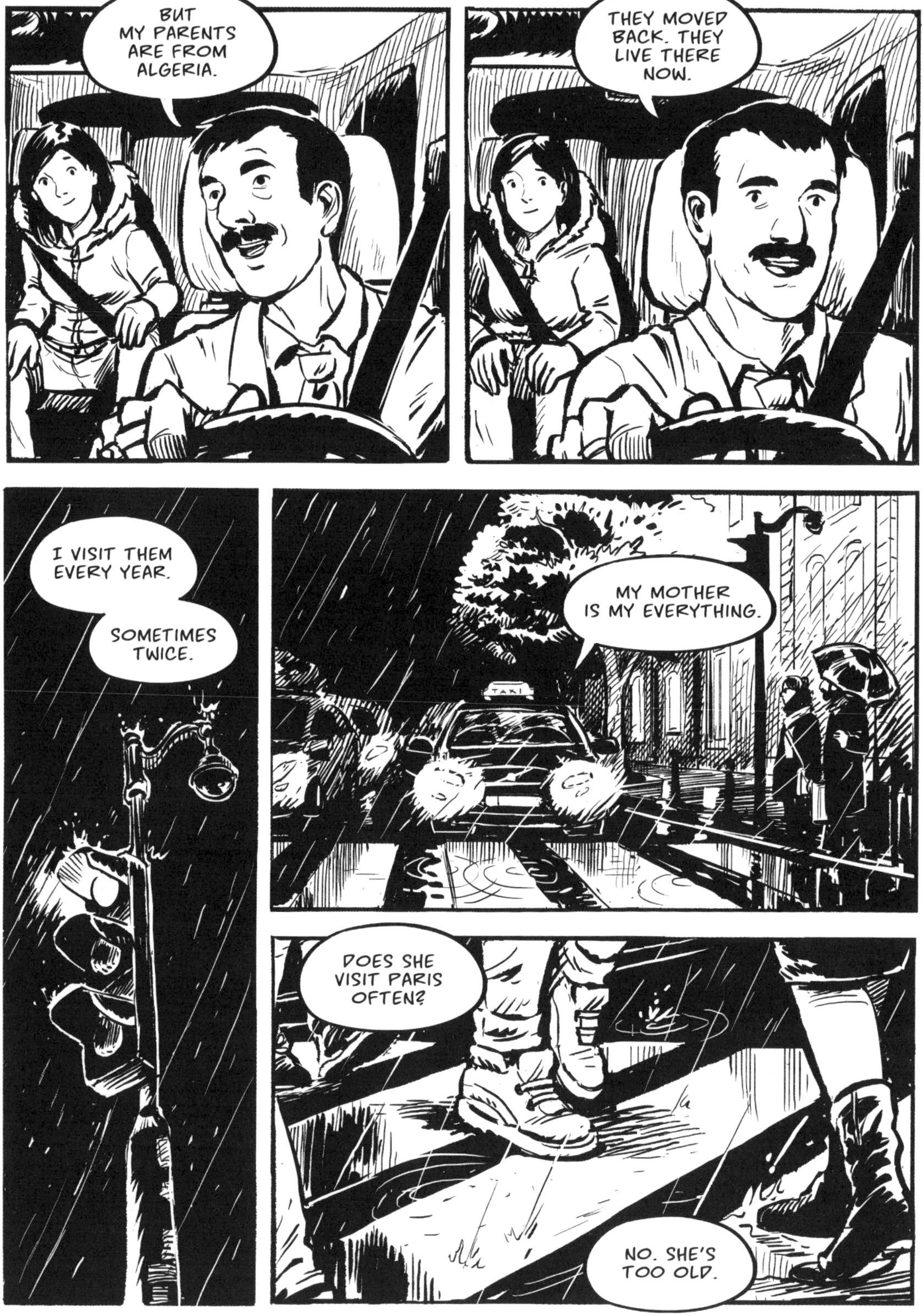
BUT MY PARENTS ARE FROM ALGERIA.
THEY MOVED BACK. THEY LIVE THERE NOW.
I VISIT THEM EVERY YEAR.
SOMETIMES TWICE.
MY MOTHER IS MY EVERYTHING.
TAXI
DOES SHE VISIT PARIS OFTEN?
NO. SHE'S TOO OLD.

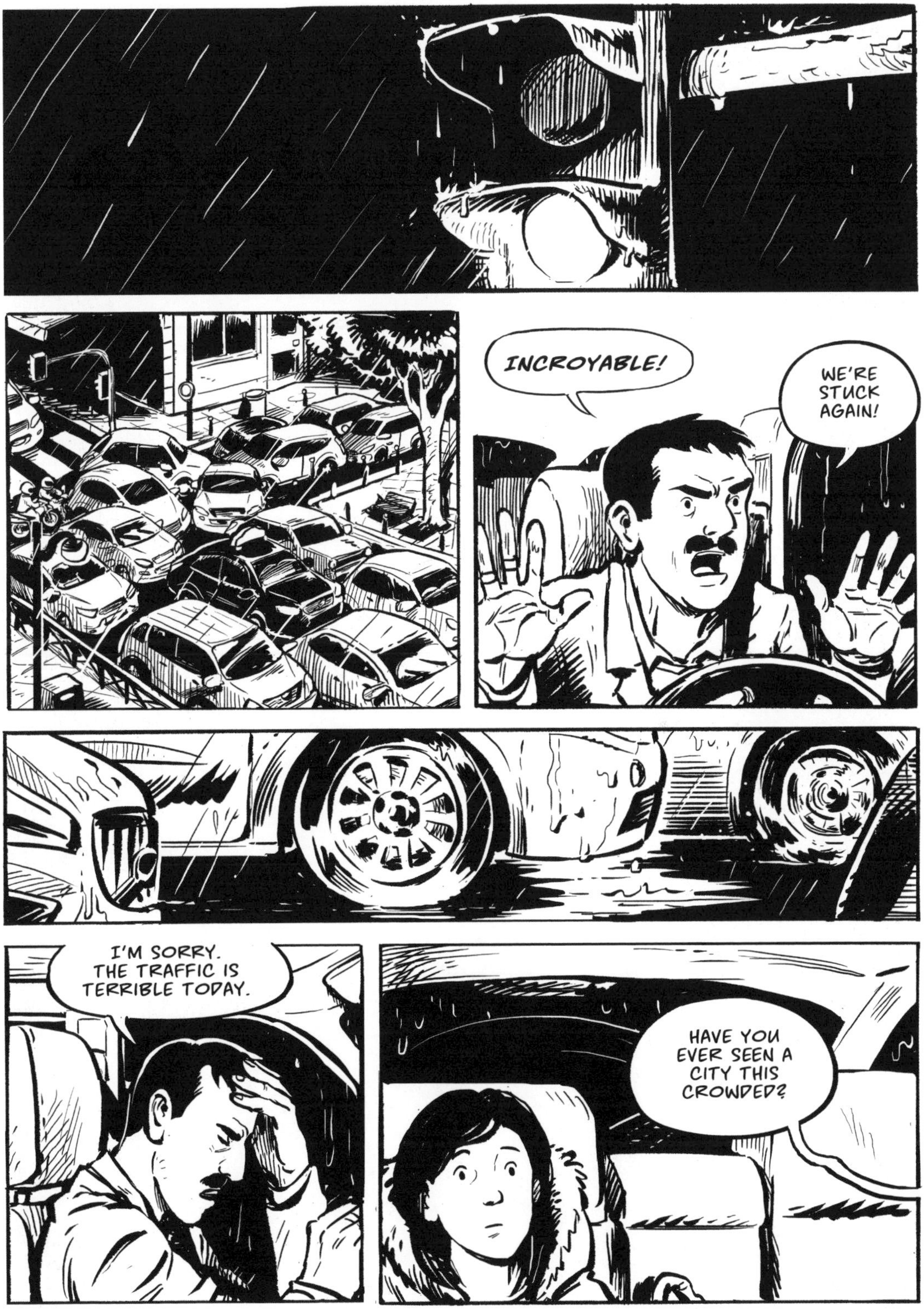
INCROYABLE!
WE'RE STUCK AGAIN!
I'M SORRY. THE TRAFFIC IS TERRIBLE TODAY.
HAVE YOU EVER SEEN A CITY THIS CROWDED?

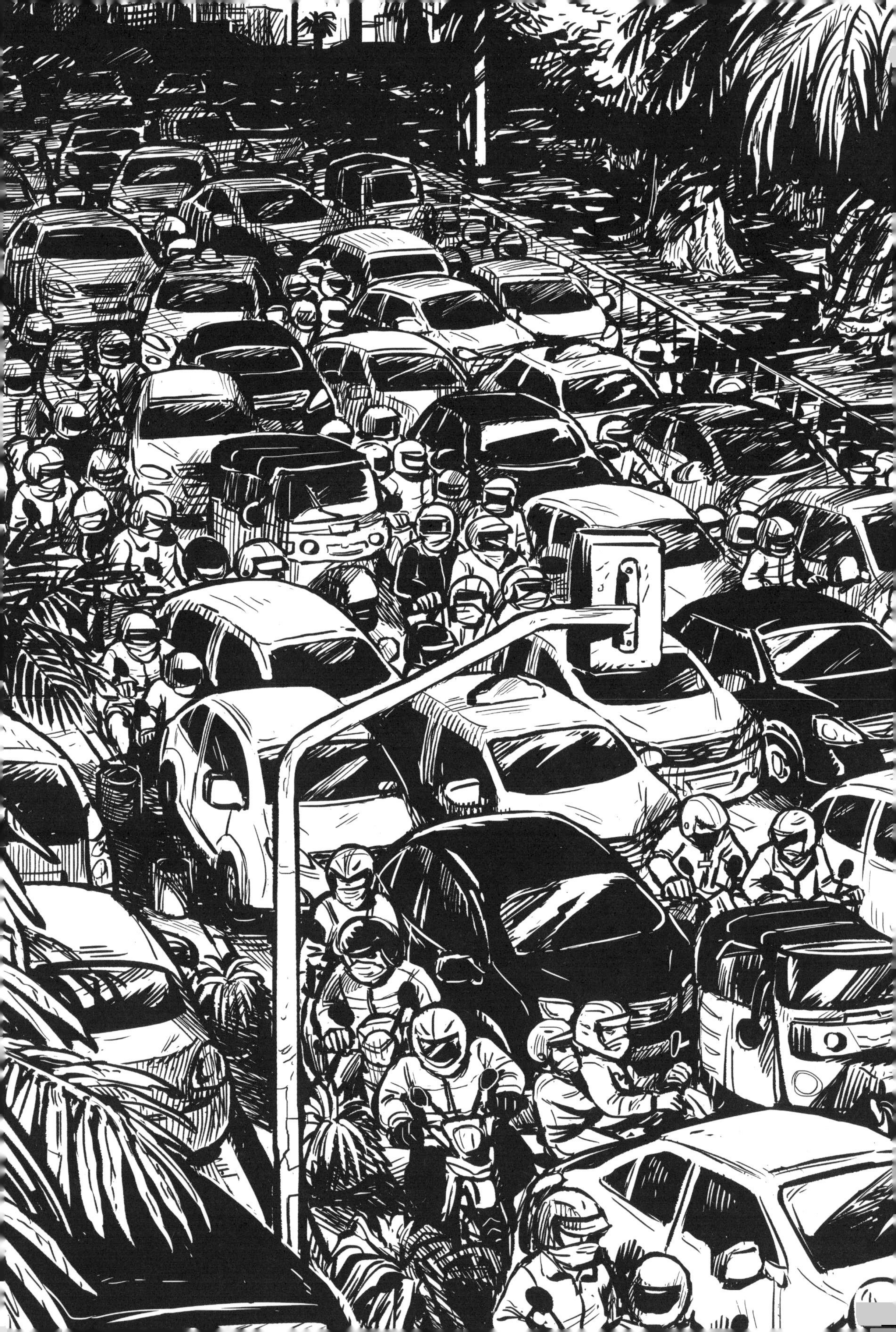

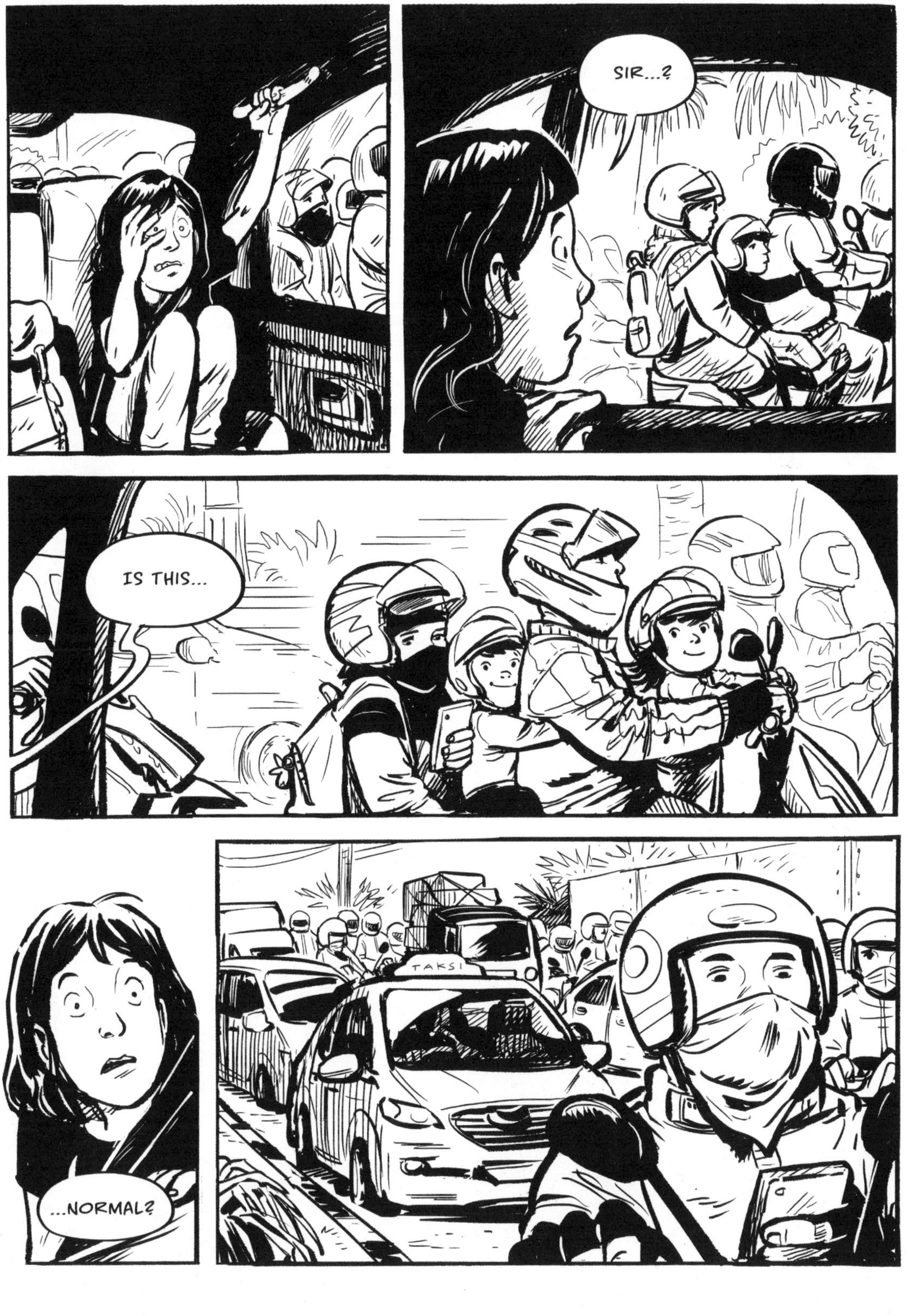
SIR...?
IS THIS...
TAKSI
...NORMAL?

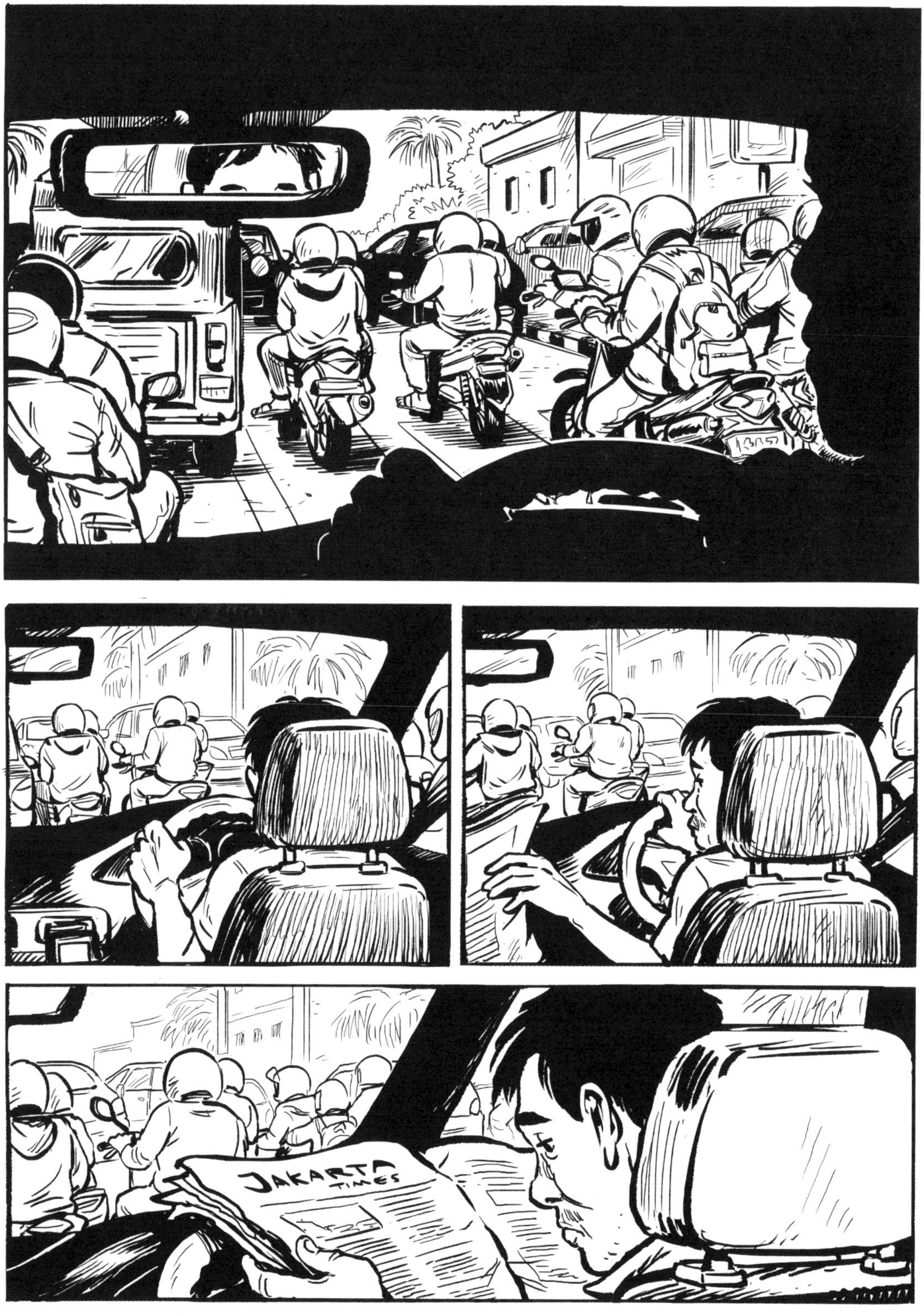
JAKARTA
TIMES

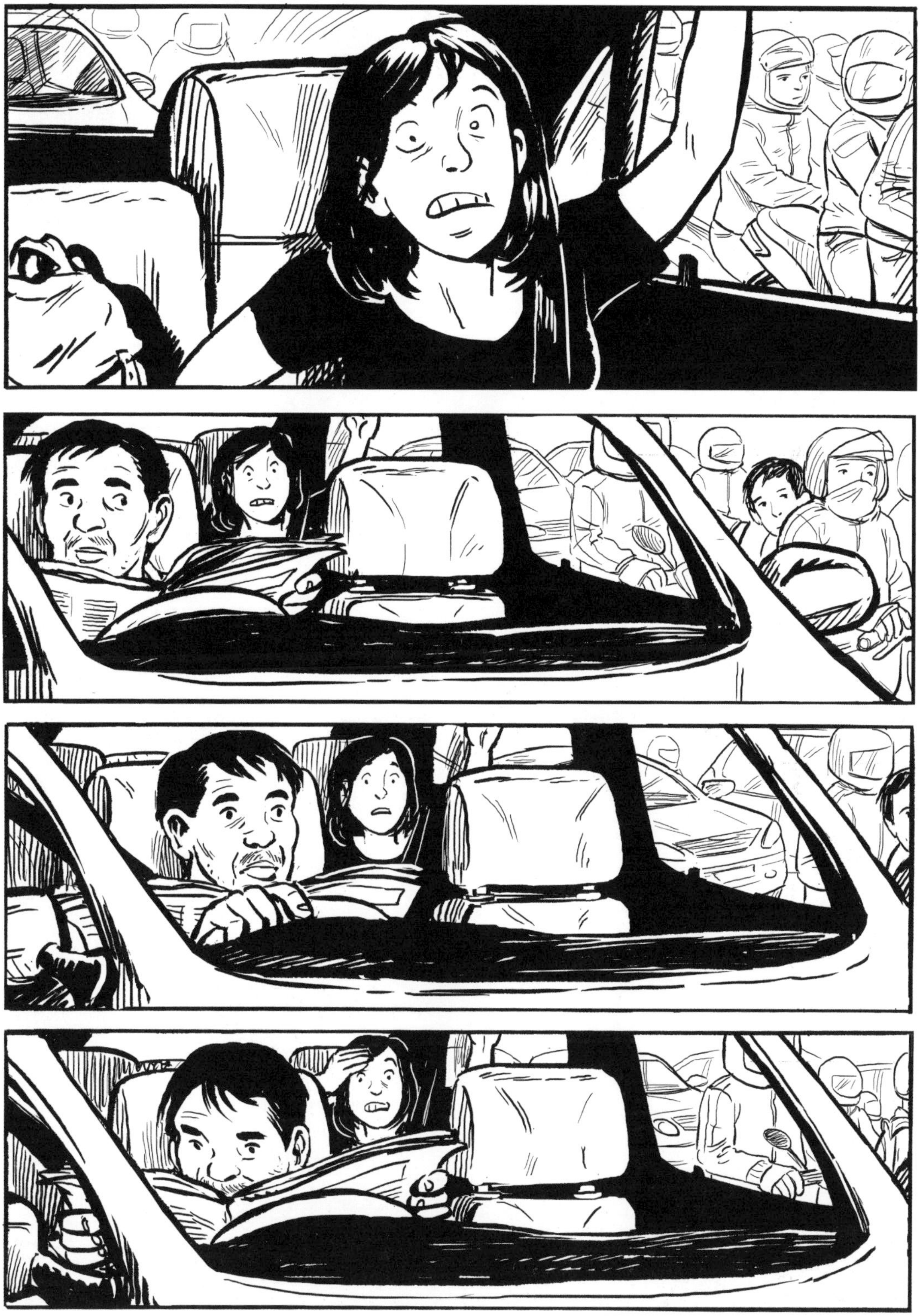

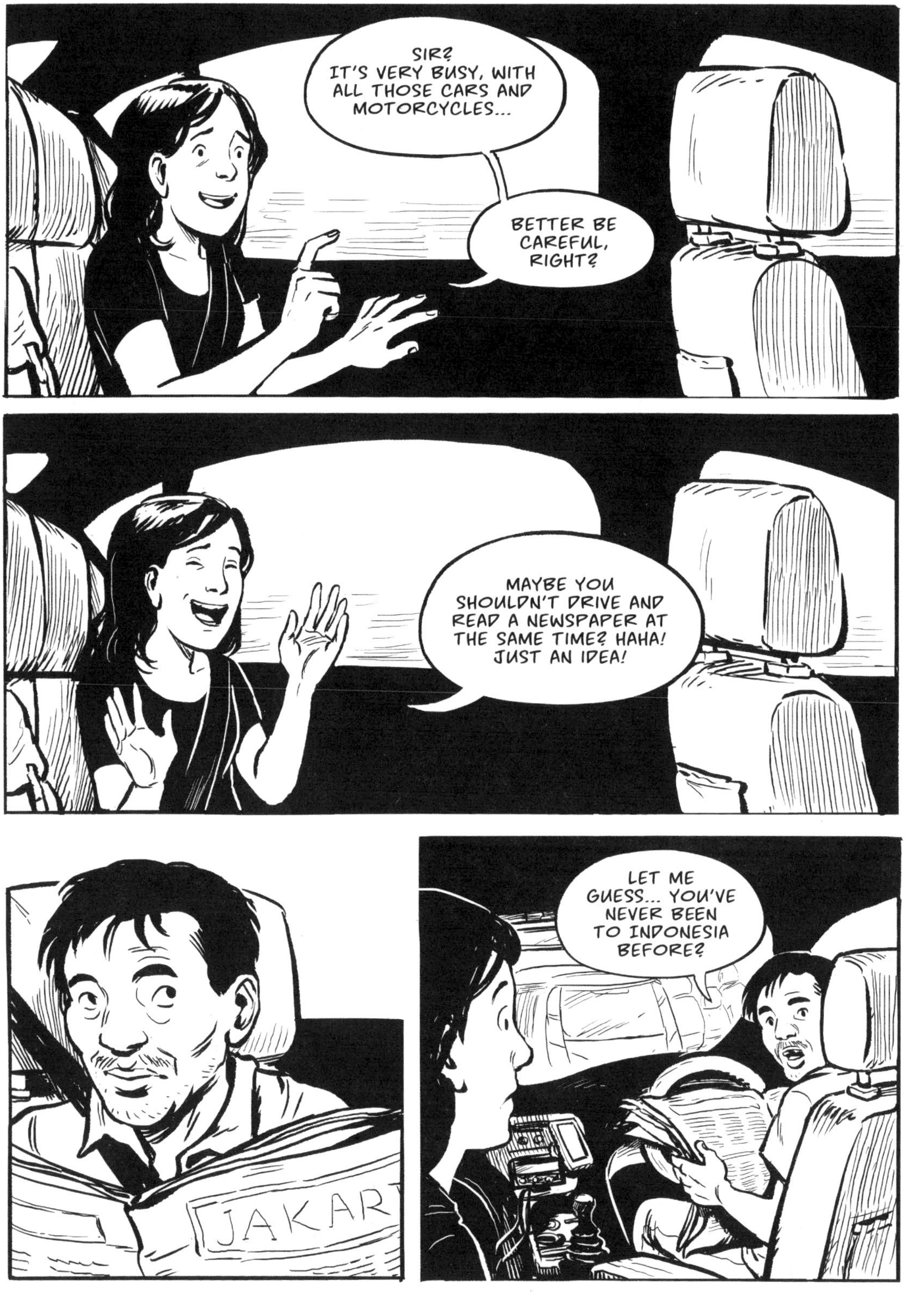
SIR? IT'S VERY BUSY, WITH ALL THOSE CARS AND MOTORCYCLES...
BETTER BE CAREFUL, RIGHT?
MAYBE YOU SHOULDN'T DRIVE AND READ A NEWSPAPER AT THE SAME TIME? HAHA! JUST AN IDEA!
JAKART
LET ME GUESS... YOU'VE NEVER BEEN TO INDONESIA BEFORE?

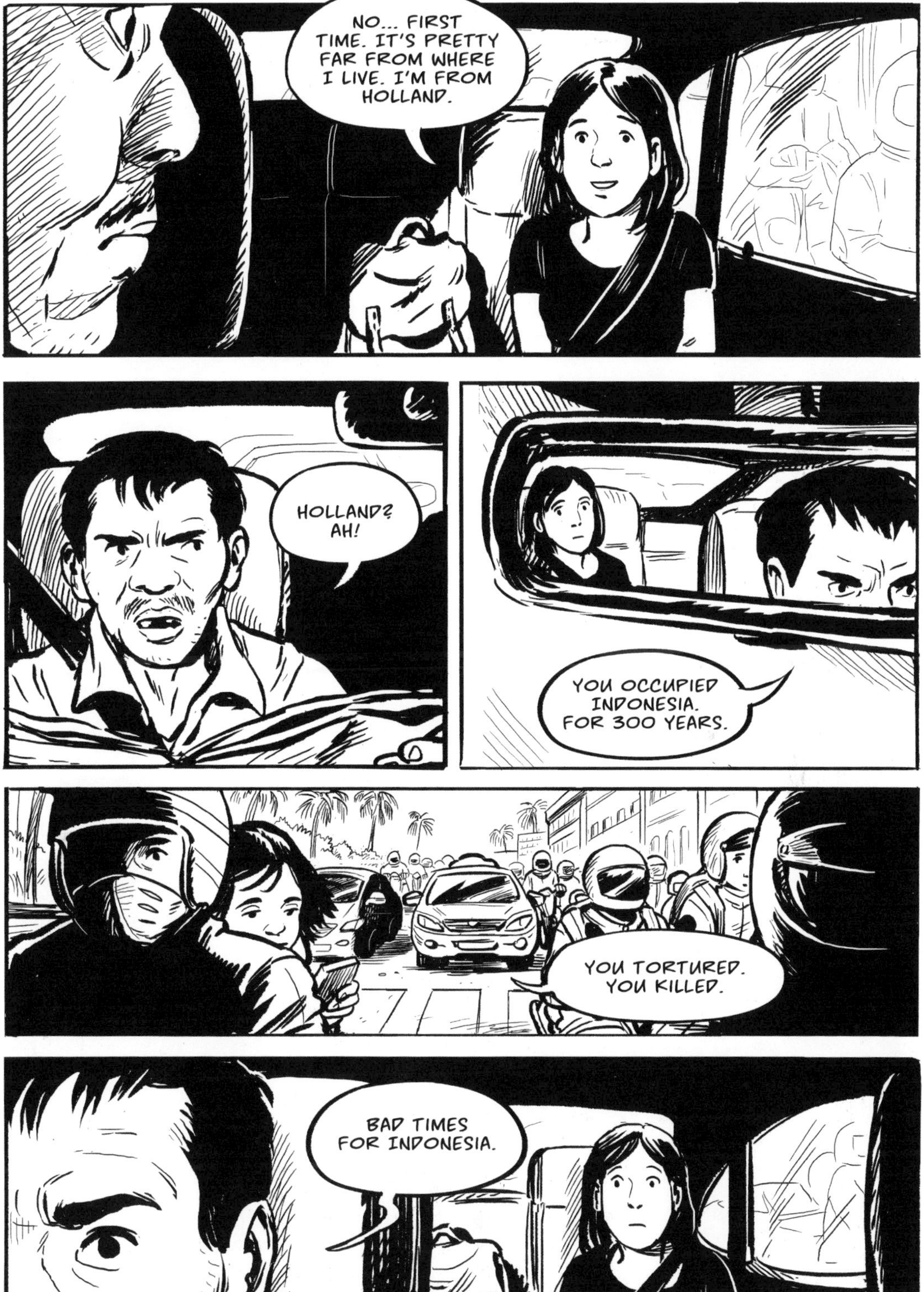
NO... FIRST TIME. IT'S PRETTY FAR FROM WHERE I LIVE. I'M FROM HOLLAND.
HOLLAND? AH!
YOU OCCUPIED INDONESIA. FOR 300 YEARS.
YOU TORTURED. YOU KILLED.
BAD TIMES FOR INDONESIA.

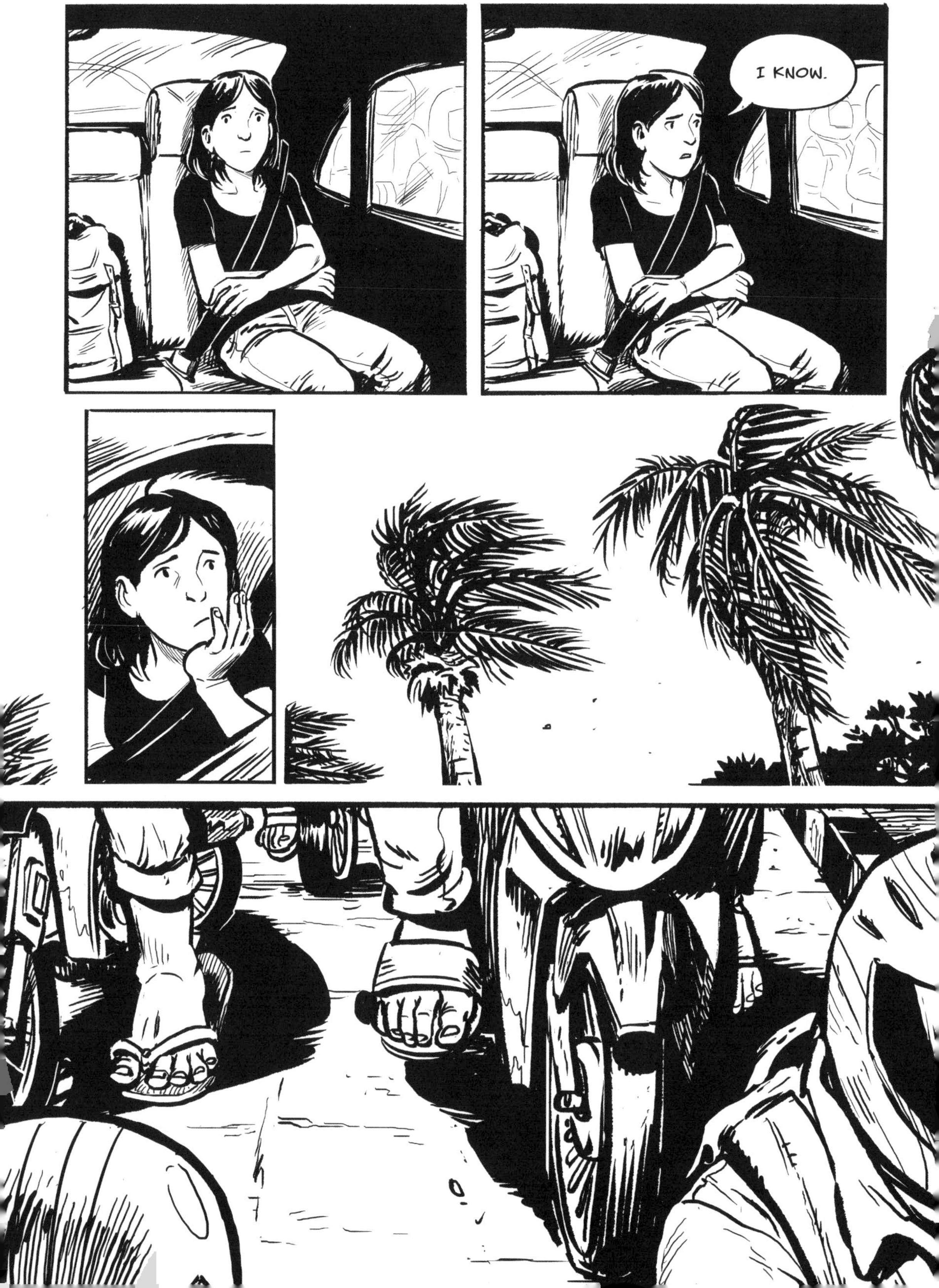
I KNOW.

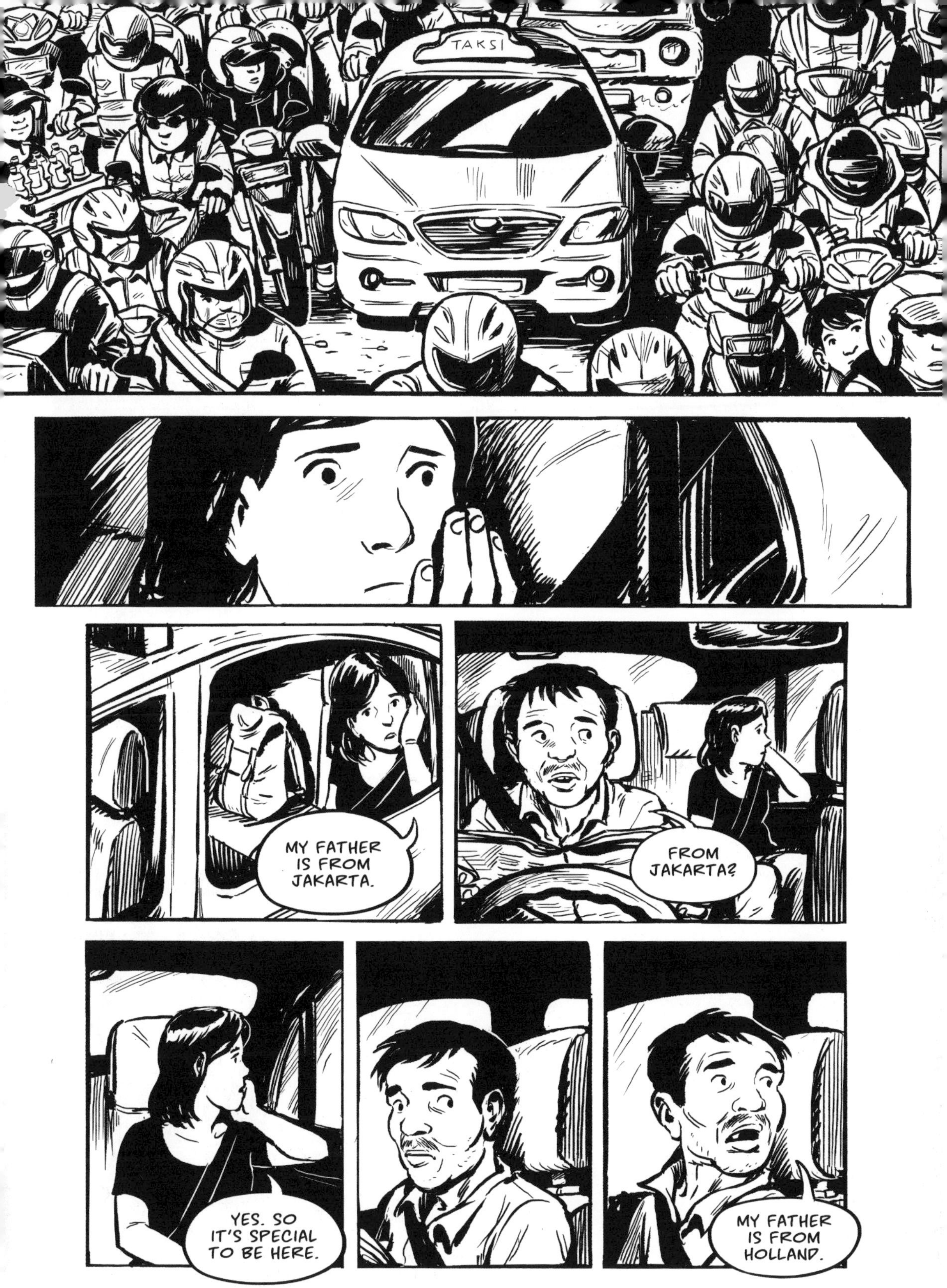
TAKSI
MY FATHER IS FROM JAKARTA.
FROM JAKARTA?
YES. SO IT'S SPECIAL TO BE HERE.
MY FATHER IS FROM HOLLAND.

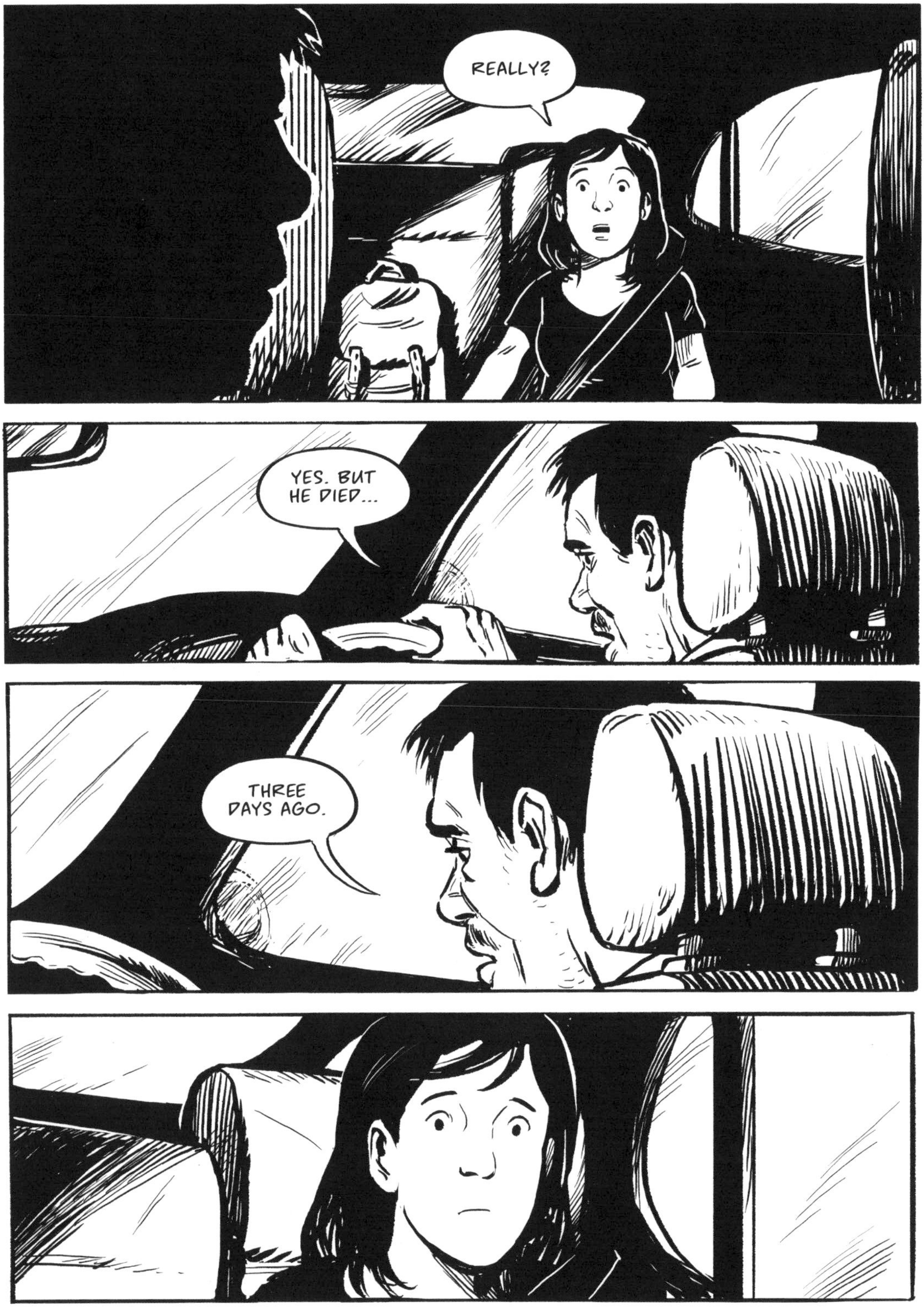
REALLY?
YES. BUT HE DIED...
THREE DAYS AGO.

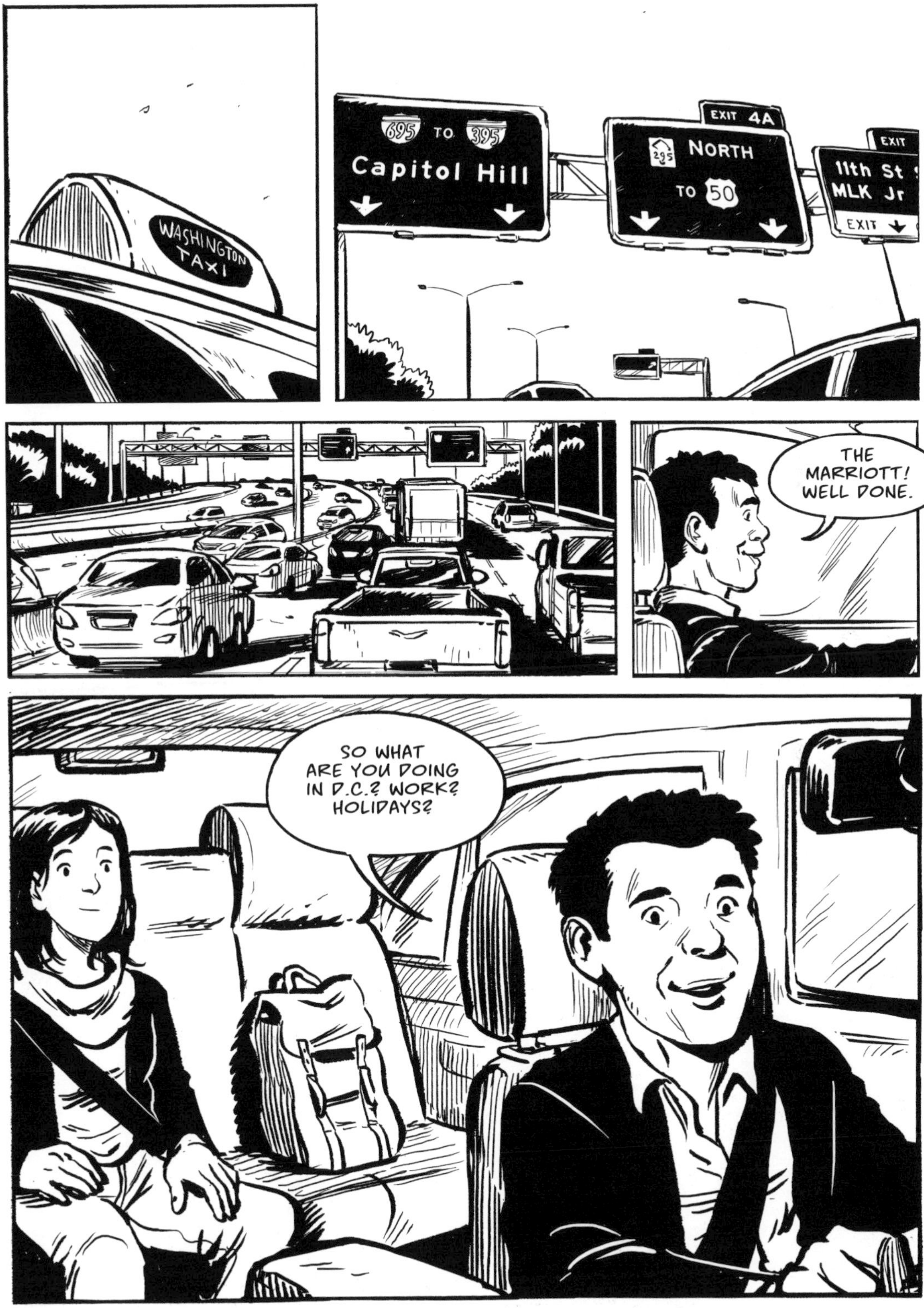
WASHINGTON TAXI
695 TO 395
Capitol Hill
EXIT 4A
295 NORTH
TO 50
EXIT
11th St
MLK Jr
EXIT
THE MARRIOTT! WELL DONE.
SO WHAT ARE YOU DOING IN D.C.? WORK? HOLIDAYS?

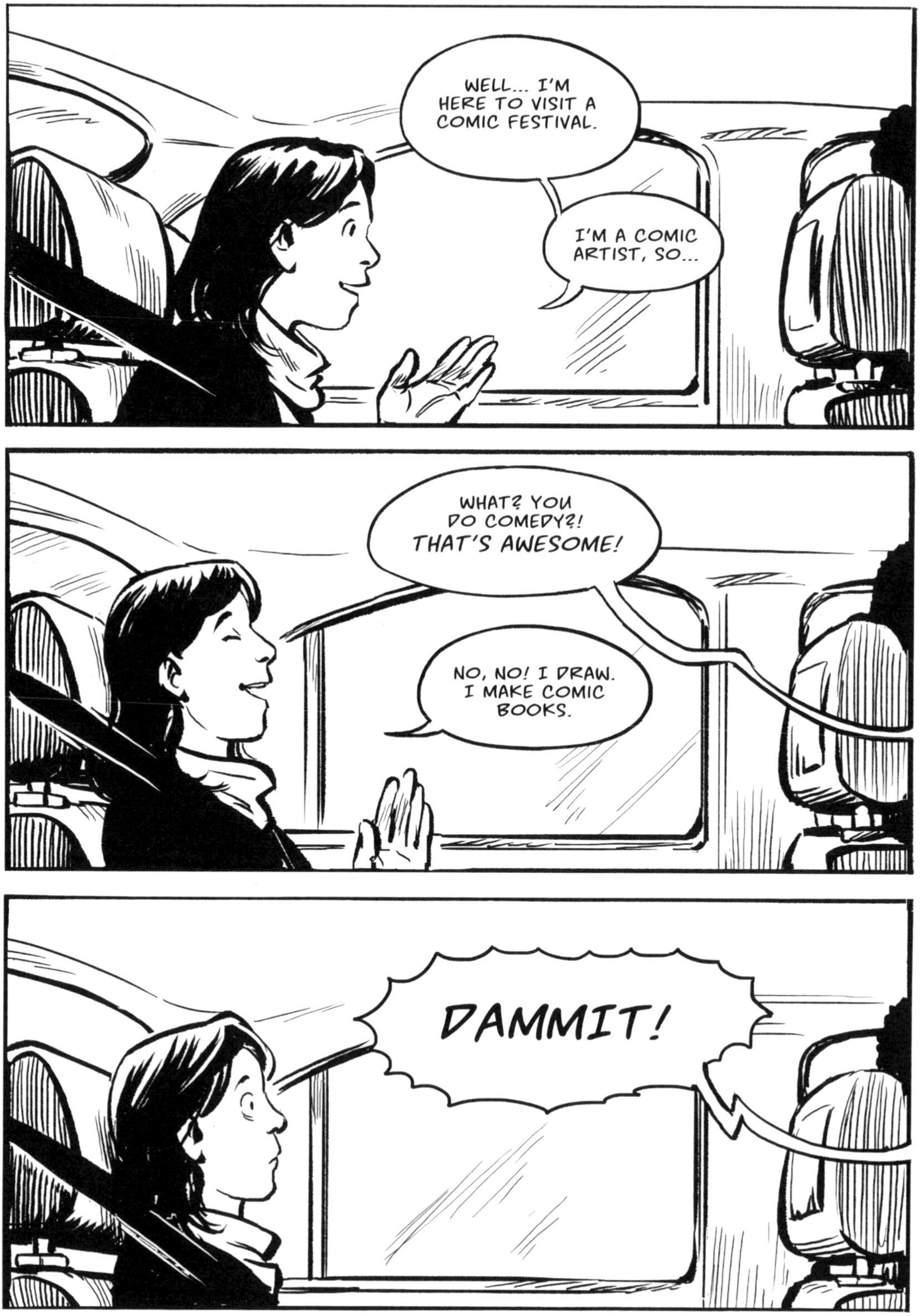
WELL... I'M HERE TO VISIT A COMIC FESTIVAL.
I'M A COMIC ARTIST, SO...
WHAT? YOU DO COMEDY?! THAT'S AWESOME!
NO, NO! I DRAW. I MAKE COMIC BOOKS.
DAMMIT!

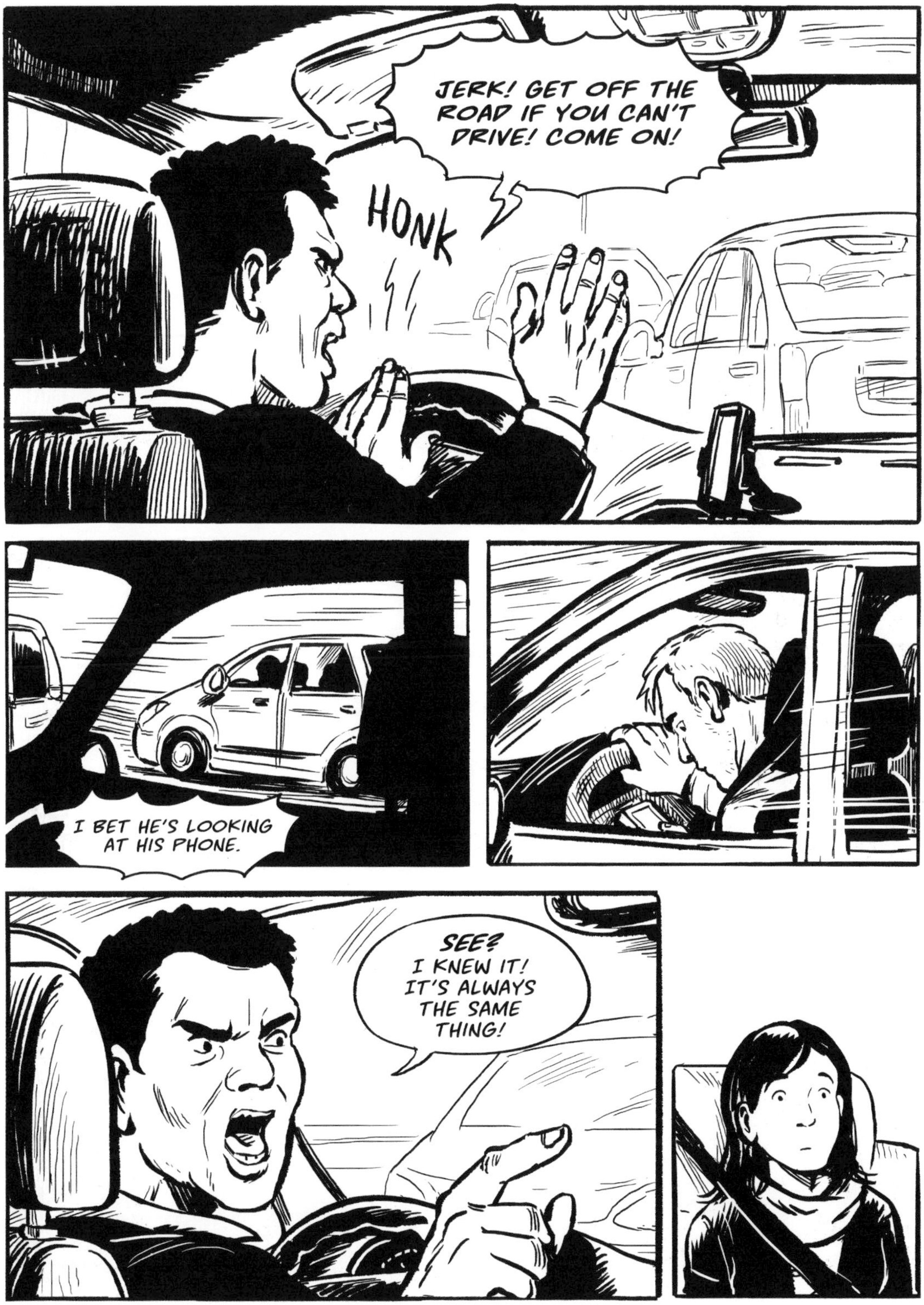
JERK! GET OFF THE ROAD IF YOU CAN'T DRIVE! COME ON!
HONK
I BET HE'S LOOKING AT HIS PHONE.
SEE? I KNEW IT! IT'S ALWAYS THE SAME THING!

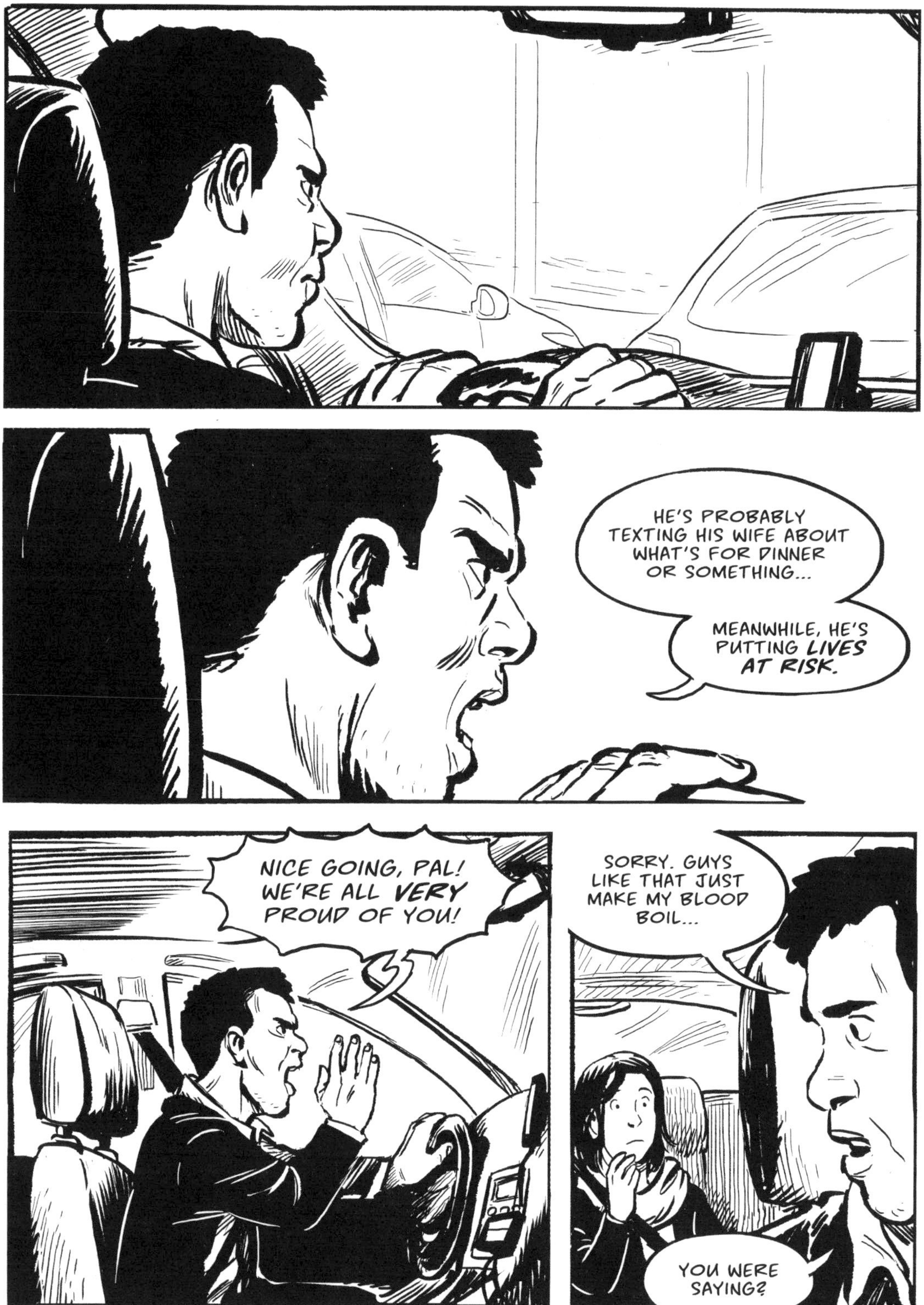
HE'S PROBABLY TEXTING HIS WIFE ABOUT WHAT'S FOR DINNER OR SOMETHING...
MEANWHILE, HE'S PUTTING LIVES AT RISK.
NICE GOING, PAL! WE'RE ALL VERY PROUD OF YOU!
SORRY. GUYS LIKE THAT JUST MAKE MY BLOOD BOIL...
YOU WERE SAYING?

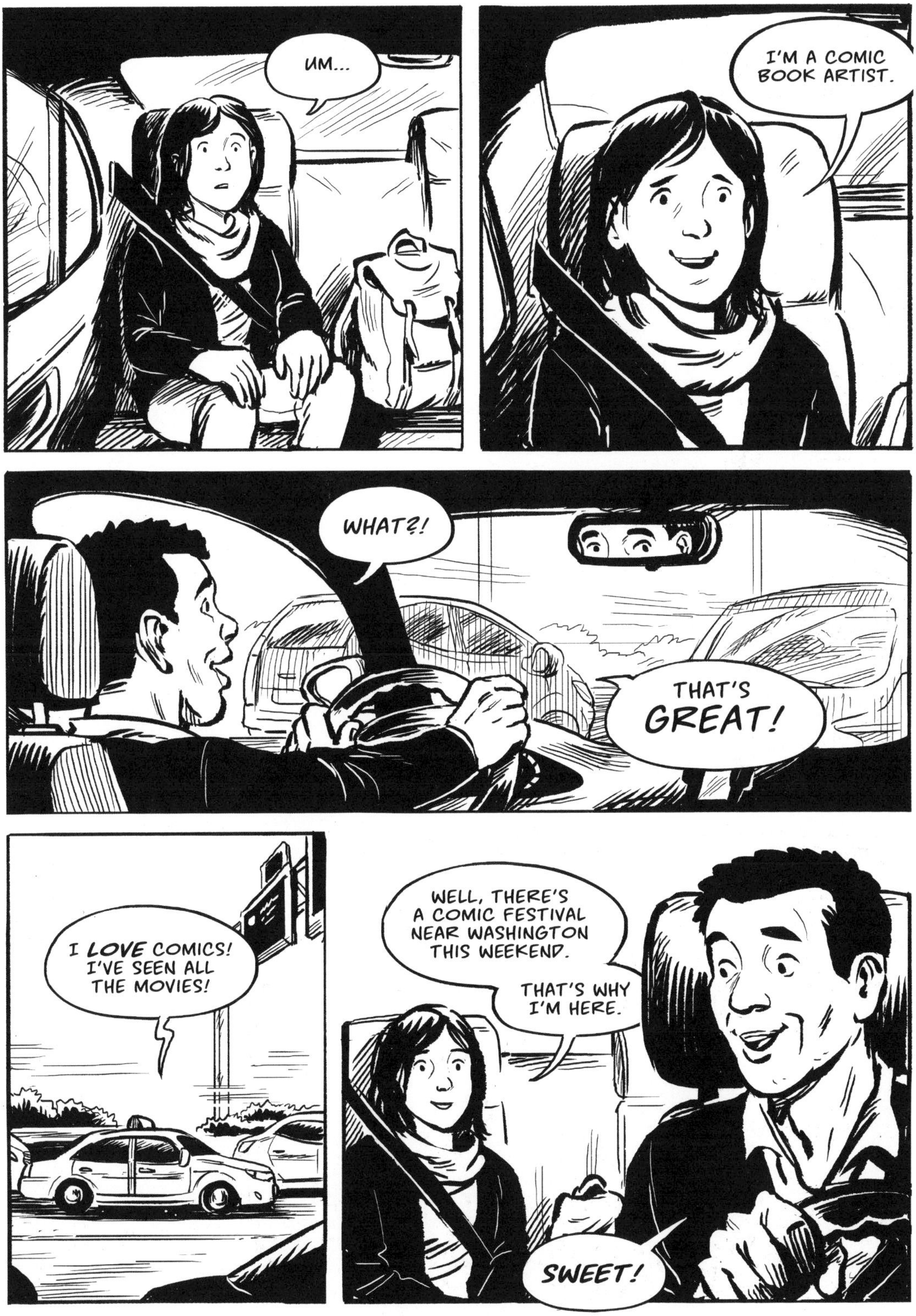
UM...
I'M A COMIC BOOK ARTIST.
WHAT?!
THAT'S GREAT!
I LOVE COMICS! I'VE SEEN ALL THE MOVIES!
WELL, THERE'S A COMIC FESTIVAL NEAR WASHINGTON THIS WEEKEND.
THAT'S WHY I'M HERE.
SWEET!

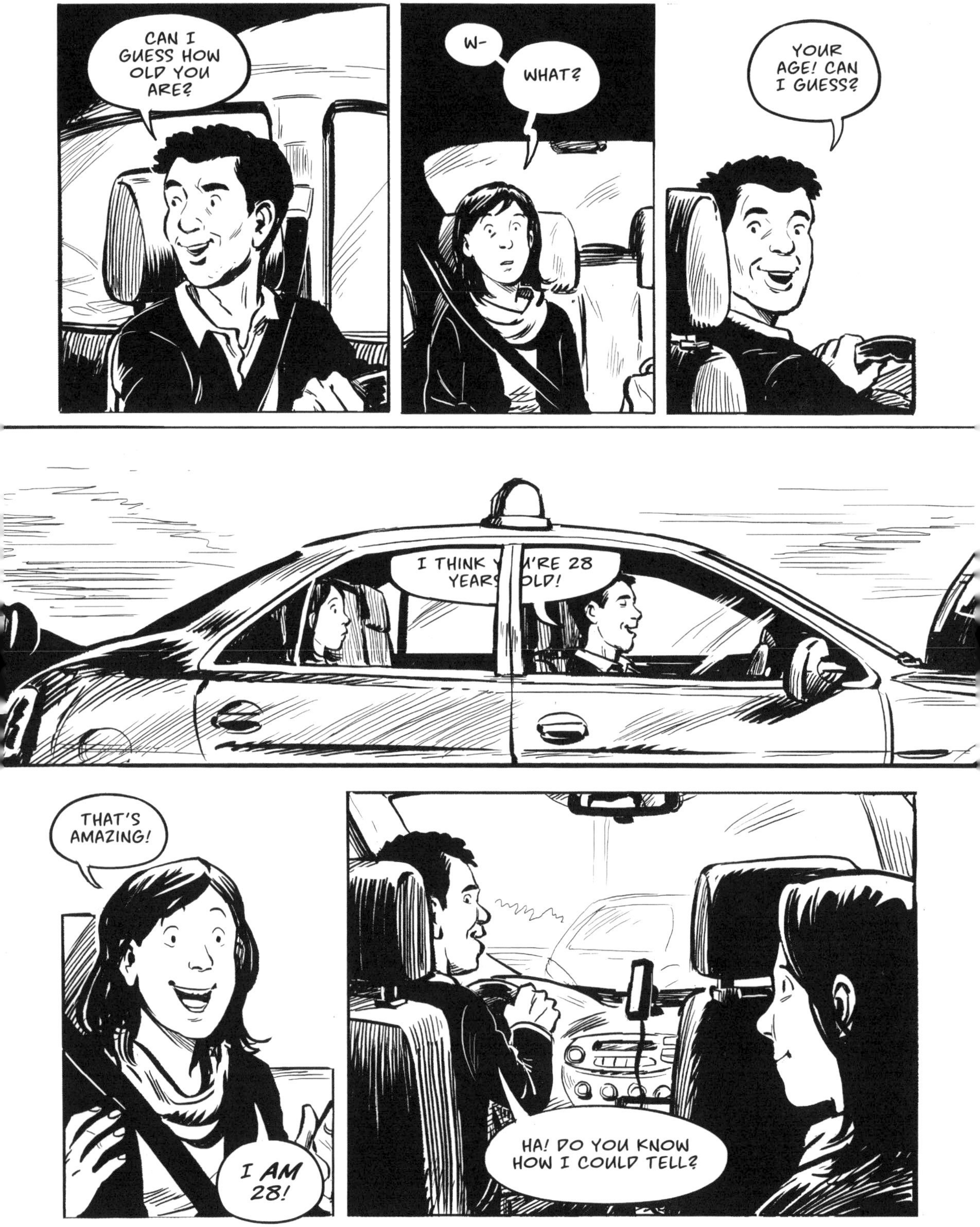
CAN I GUESS HOW OLD YOU ARE?
W-
WHAT?
YOUR AGE! CAN I GUESS?
I THINK YOU'RE 28 YEARS OLD!
THAT'S AMAZING!
I AM 28!
HA! DO YOU KNOW HOW I COULD TELL?

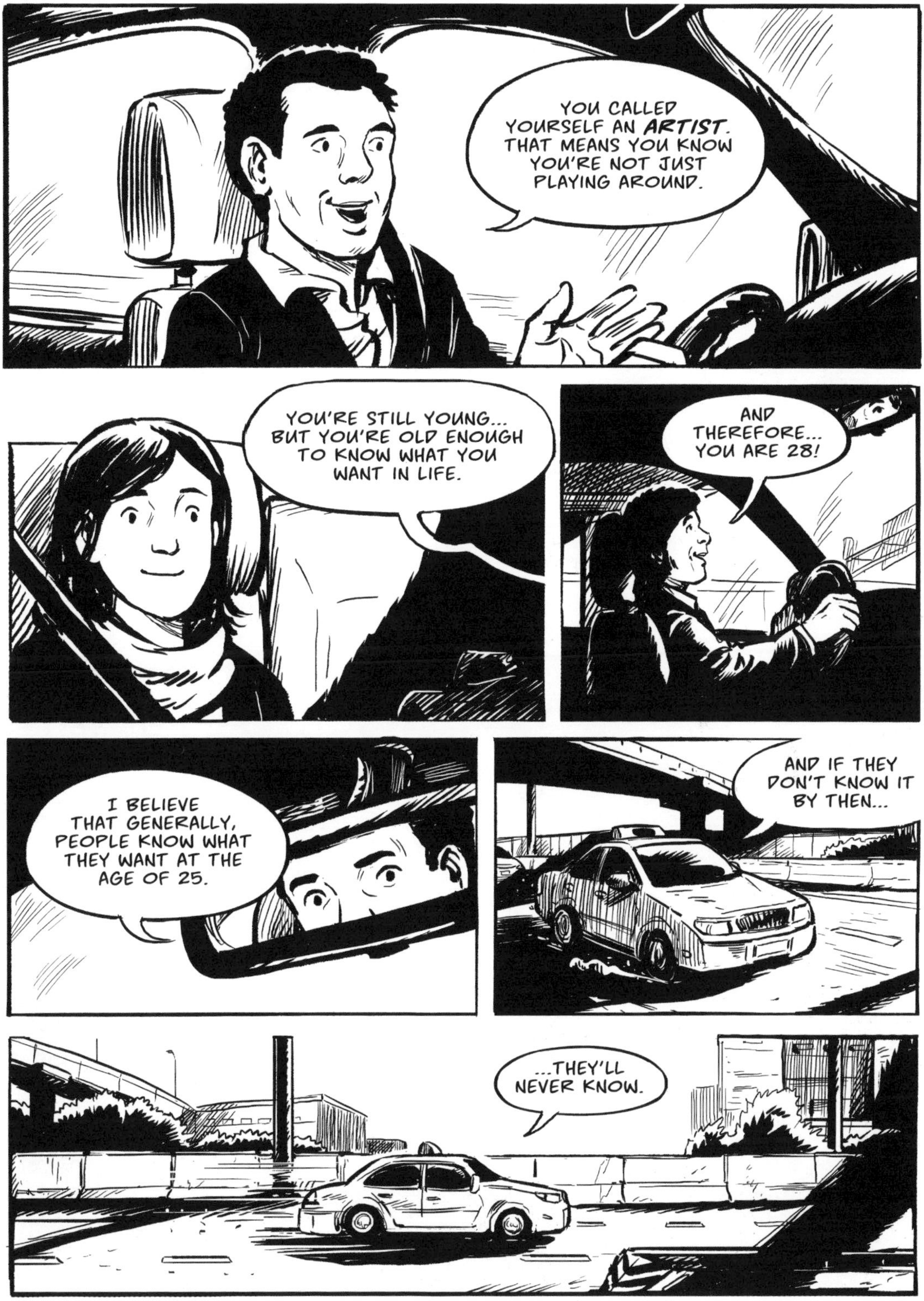
YOU CALLED YOURSELF AN ARTIST. THAT MEANS YOU KNOW YOU'RE NOT JUST PLAYING AROUND.
YOU'RE STILL YOUNG... BUT YOU'RE OLD ENOUGH TO KNOW WHAT YOU WANT IN LIFE.
AND THEREFORE... YOU ARE 28!
I BELIEVE THAT GENERALLY, PEOPLE KNOW WHAT THEY WANT AT THE AGE OF 25.
AND IF THEY DON'T KNOW IT BY THEN...
...THEY'LL NEVER KNOW.

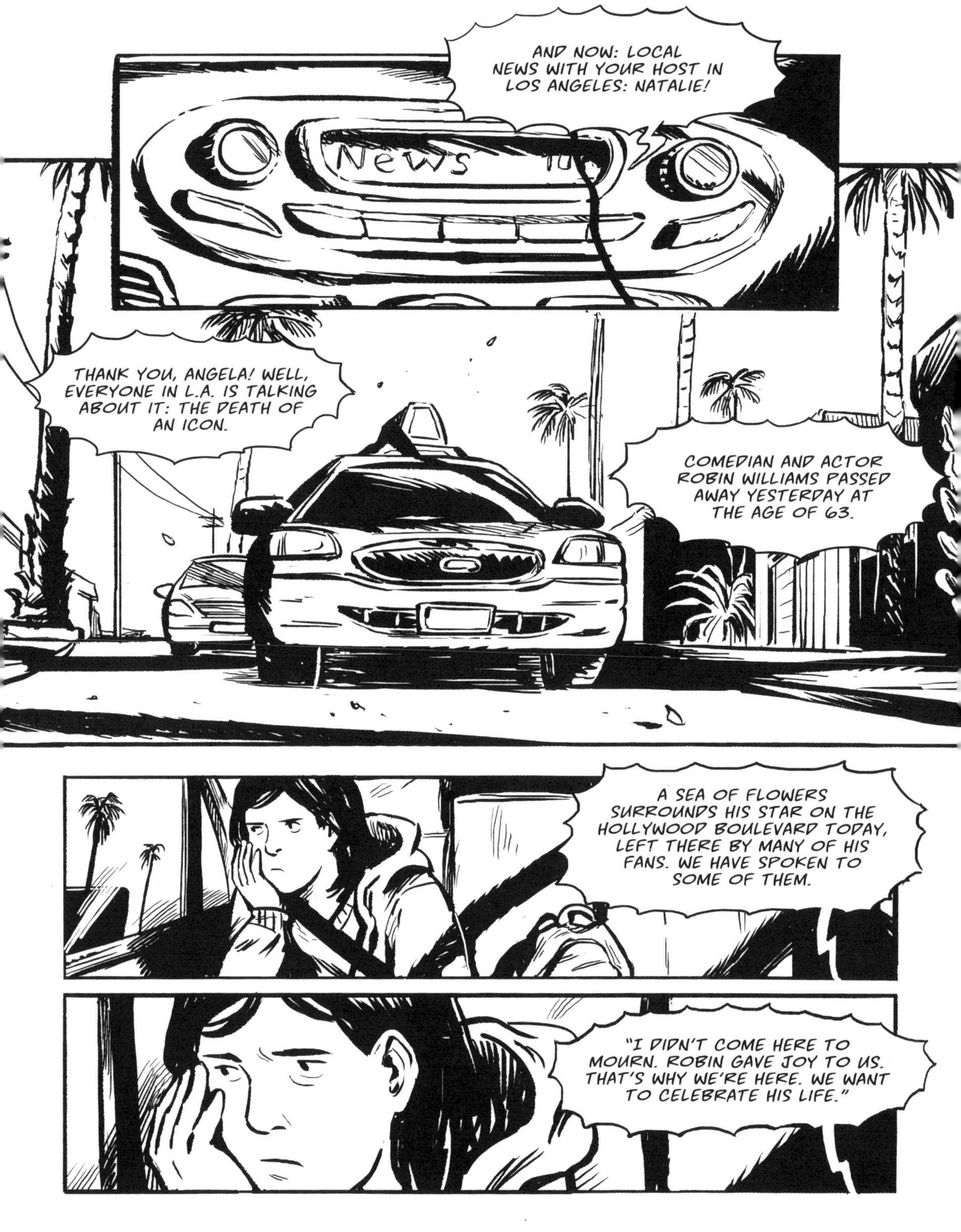
AND NOW: LOCAL NEWS WITH YOUR HOST IN LOS ANGELES: NATALIE!
NEWS
THANK YOU, ANGELA! WELL, EVERYONE IN L.A. IS TALKING ABOUT IT: THE DEATH OF AN ICON.
COMEDIAN AND ACTOR ROBIN WILLIAMS PASSED AWAY YESTERDAY AT THE AGE OF 63.
A SEA OF FLOWERS SURROUNDS HIS STAR ON THE HOLLYWOOD BOULEVARD TODAY, LEFT THERE BY MANY OF HIS FANS. WE HAVE SPOKEN TO SOME OF THEM.
"I DIDN'T COME HERE TO MOURN. ROBIN GAVE JOY TO US. THAT'S WHY WE'RE HERE. WE WANT TO CELEBRATE HIS LIFE."

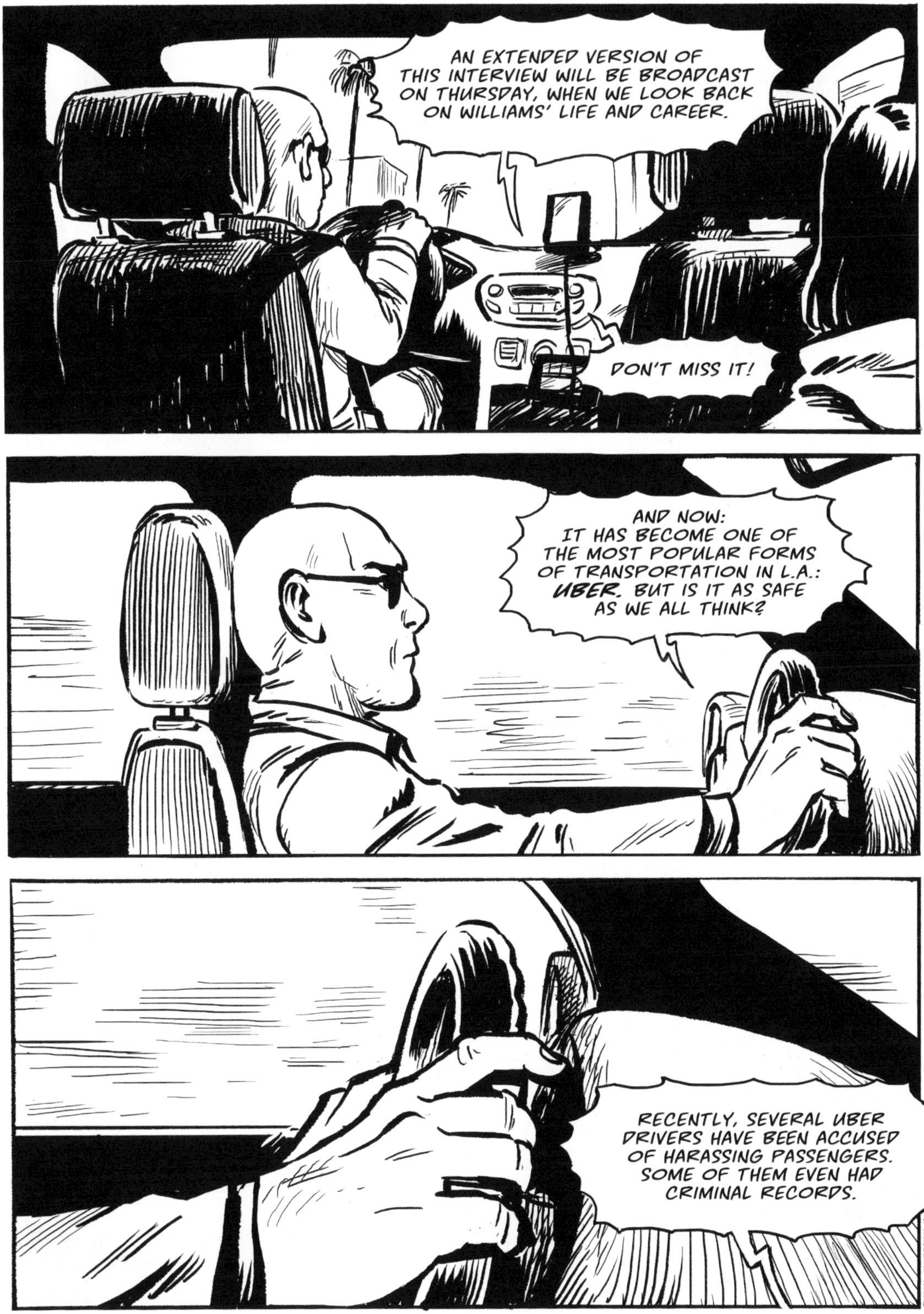
AN EXTENDED VERSION OF THIS INTERVIEW WILL BE BROADCAST ON THURSDAY, WHEN WE LOOK BACK ON WILLIAMS' LIFE AND CAREER.
DON'T MISS IT!
AND NOW: IT HAS BECOME ONE OF THE MOST POPULAR FORMS OF TRANSPORTATION IN L.A.: UBER. BUT IS IT AS SAFE AS WE ALL THINK?
RECENTLY, SEVERAL UBER DRIVERS HAVE BEEN ACCUSED OF HARASSING PASSENGERS. SOME OF THEM EVEN HAD CRIMINAL RECORDS.

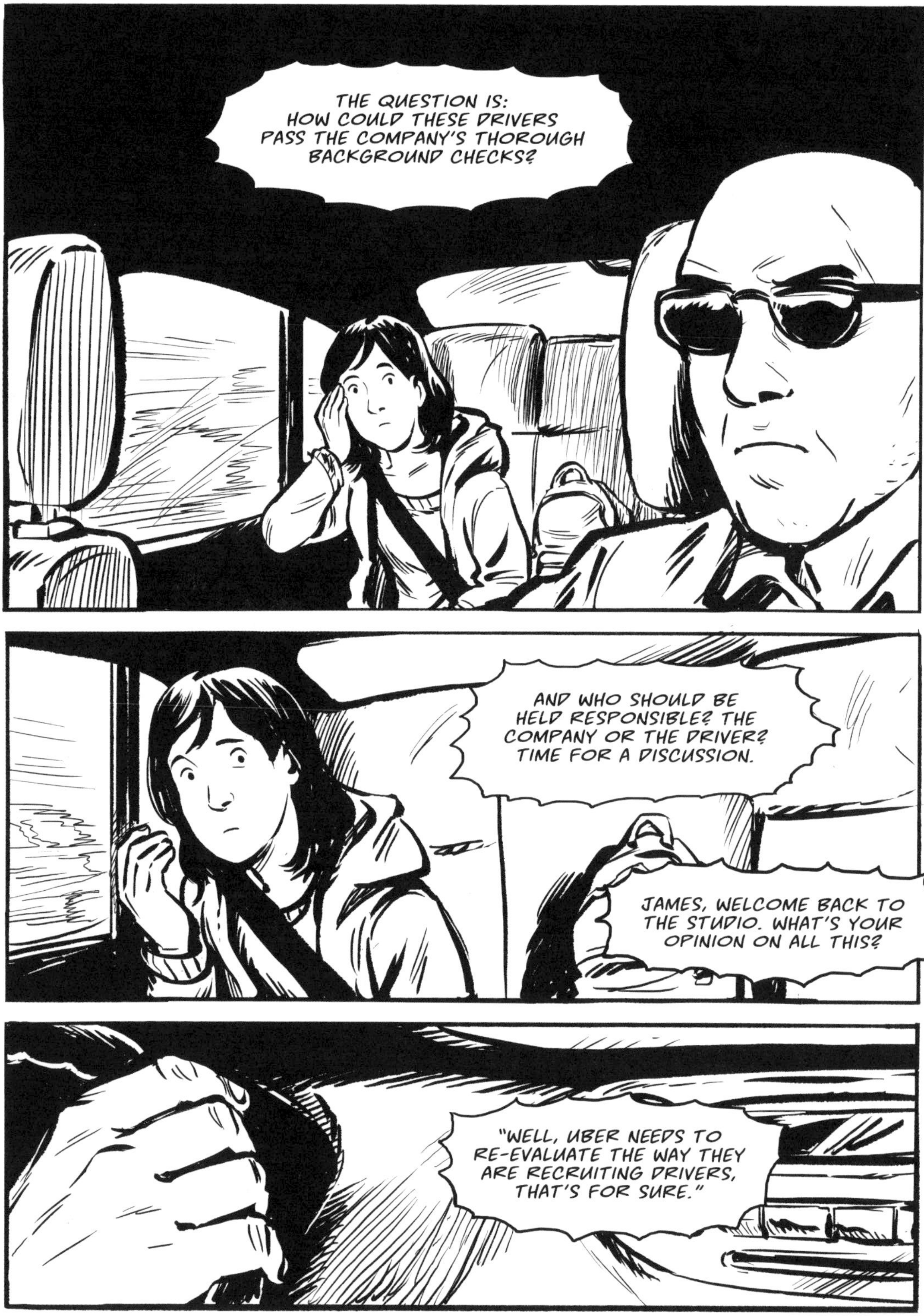
THE QUESTION IS: HOW COULD THESE DRIVERS PASS THE COMPANY'S THOROUGH BACKGROUND CHECKS?
AND WHO SHOULD BE HELD RESPONSIBLE? THE COMPANY OR THE DRIVER? TIME FOR A DISCUSSION.
JAMES, WELCOME BACK TO THE STUDIO. WHAT'S YOUR OPINION ON ALL THIS?
"WELL, UBER NEEDS TO RE-EVALUATE THE WAY THEY ARE RECRUITING DRIVERS, THAT'S FOR SURE."

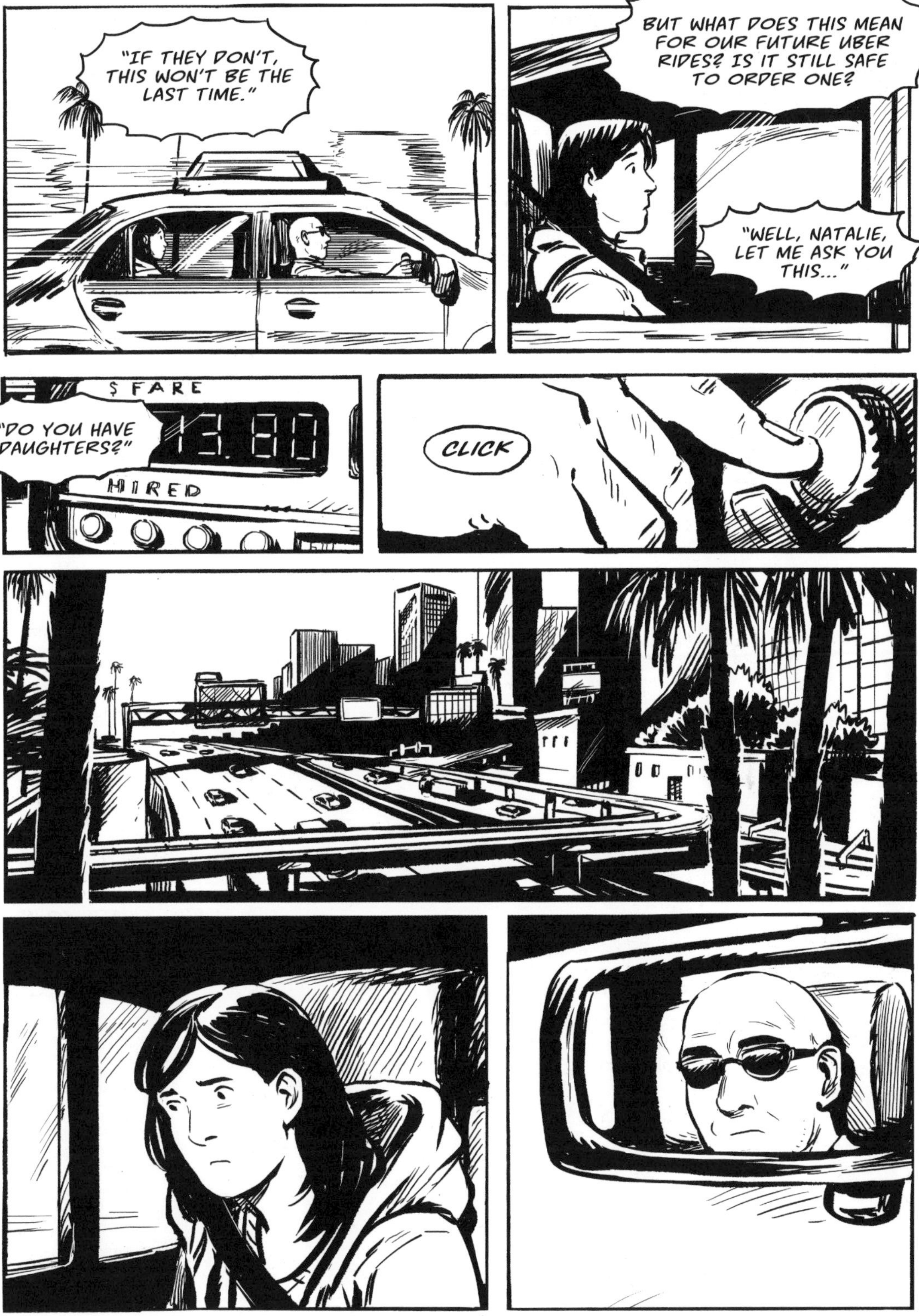
"IF THEY DON'T, THIS WON'T BE THE LAST TIME."
BUT WHAT DOES THIS MEAN FOR OUR FUTURE UBER RIDES? IS IT STILL SAFE TO ORDER ONE?
"WELL, NATALIE, LET ME ASK YOU THIS..."
$ FARE
13.80
HIRED
"DO YOU HAVE DAUGHTERS?"
CLICK

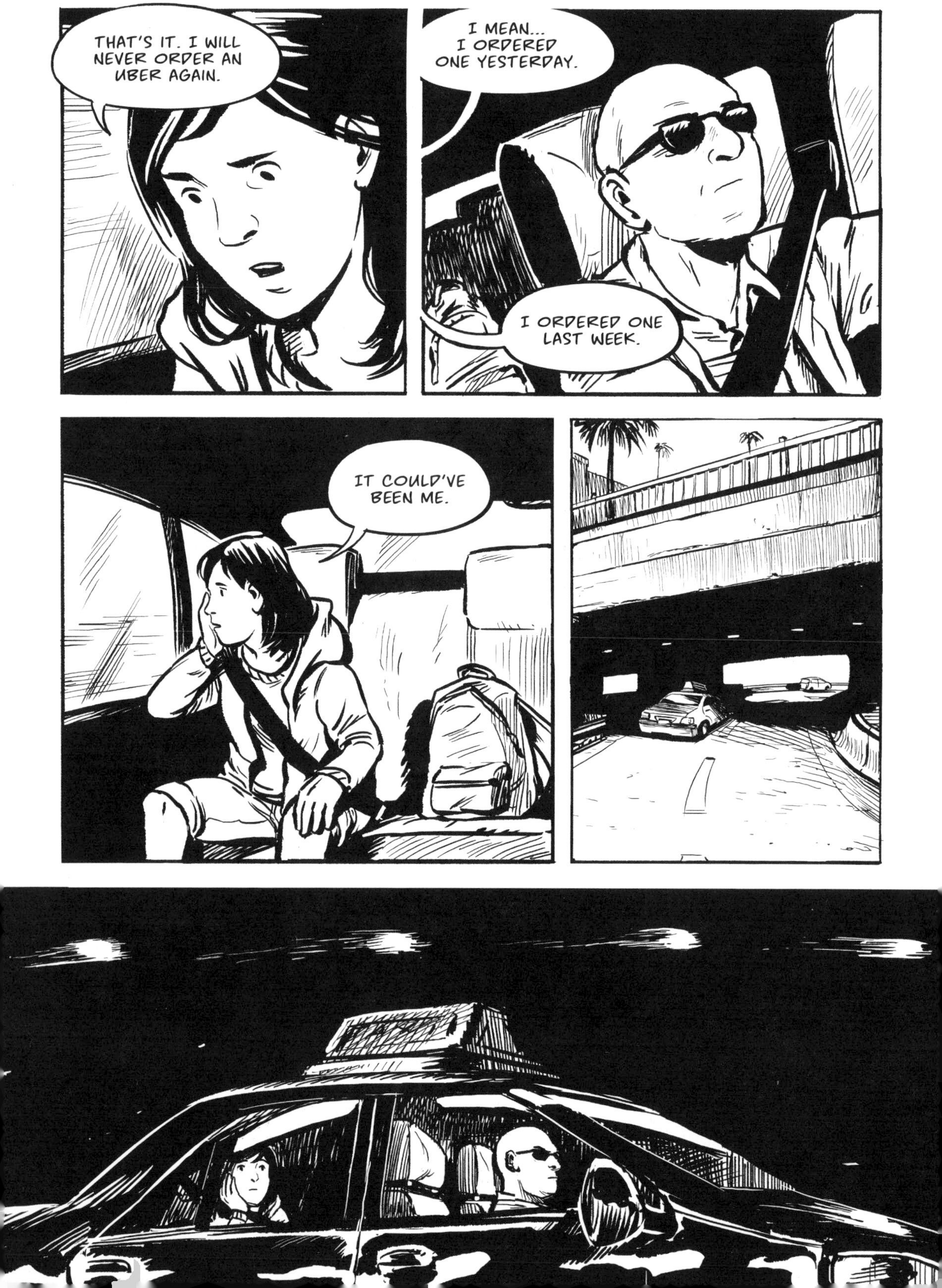
THAT'S IT. I WILL NEVER ORDER AN UBER AGAIN.
I MEAN... I ORDERED ONE YESTERDAY.
I ORDERED ONE LAST WEEK.
IT COULD'VE BEEN ME.

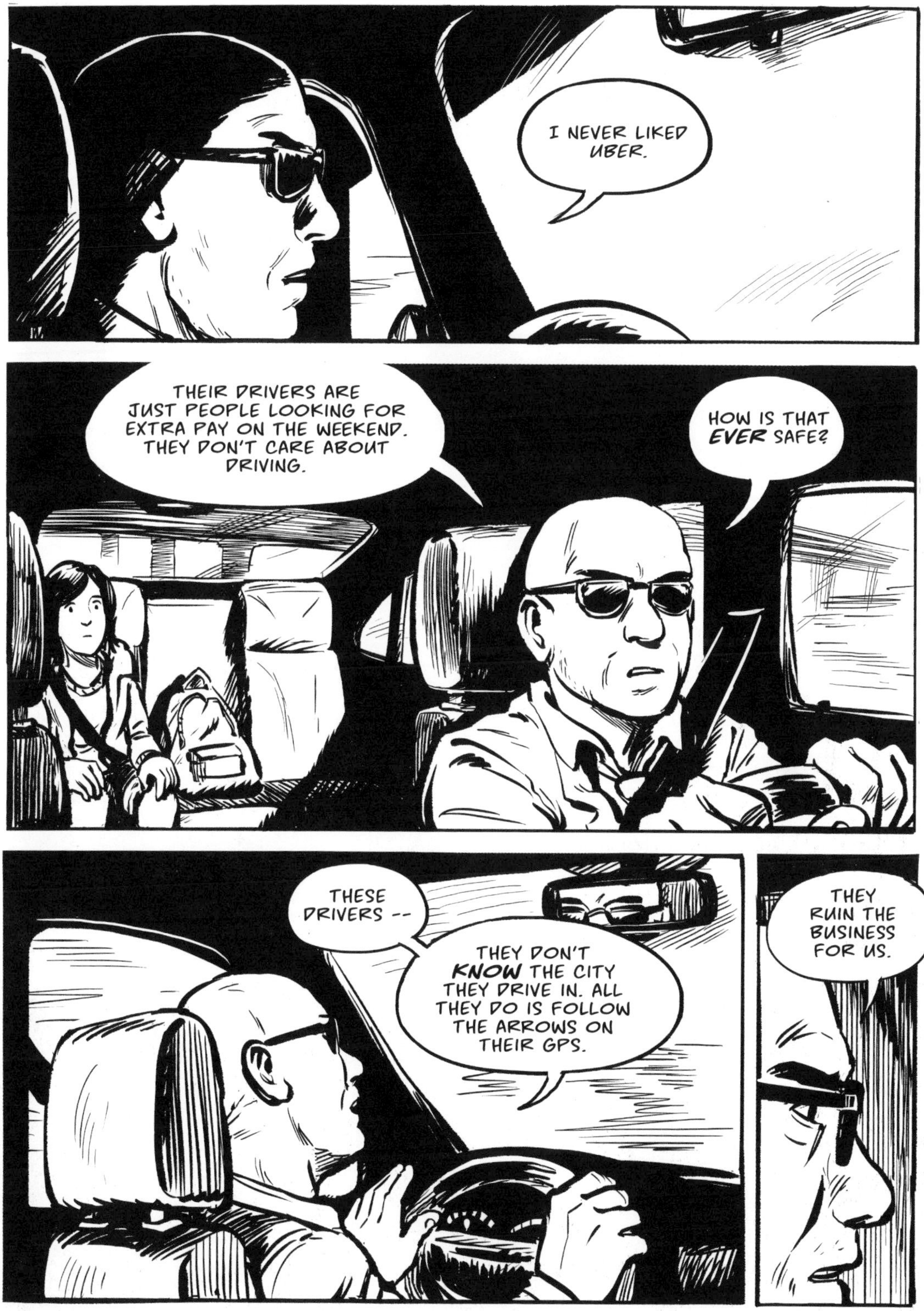
I NEVER LIKED UBER.
THEIR DRIVERS ARE JUST PEOPLE LOOKING FOR EXTRA PAY ON THE WEEKEND. THEY DON'T CARE ABOUT DRIVING.
HOW IS THAT *EVER* SAFE?
THESE DRIVERS --
THEY DON'T *KNOW* THE CITY THEY DRIVE IN. ALL THEY DO IS FOLLOW THE ARROWS ON THEIR GPS.
THEY RUIN THE BUSINESS FOR US.

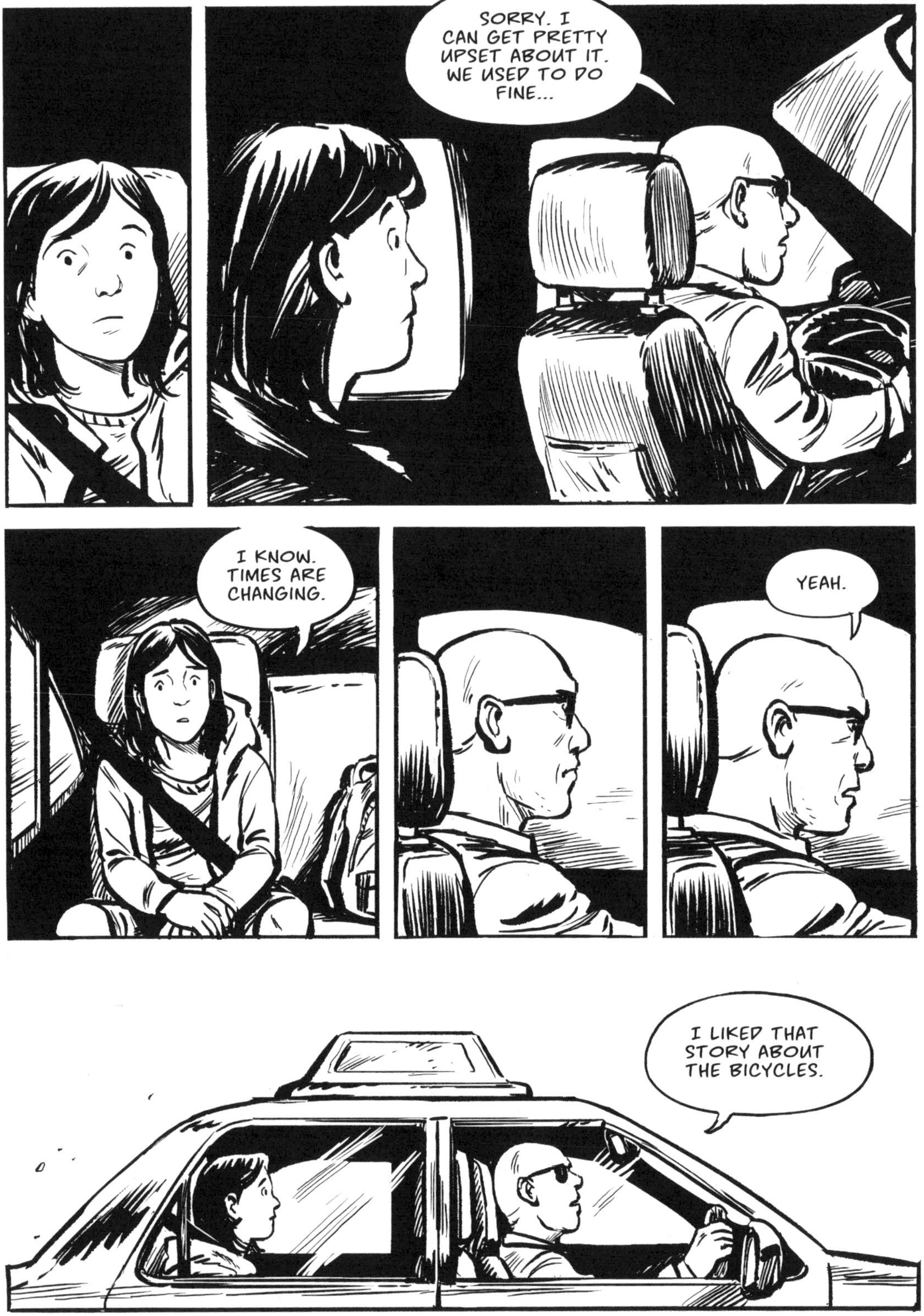
SORRY. I CAN GET PRETTY UPSET ABOUT IT. WE USED TO DO FINE...
I KNOW. TIMES ARE CHANGING.
YEAH.
I LIKED THAT STORY ABOUT THE BICYCLES.

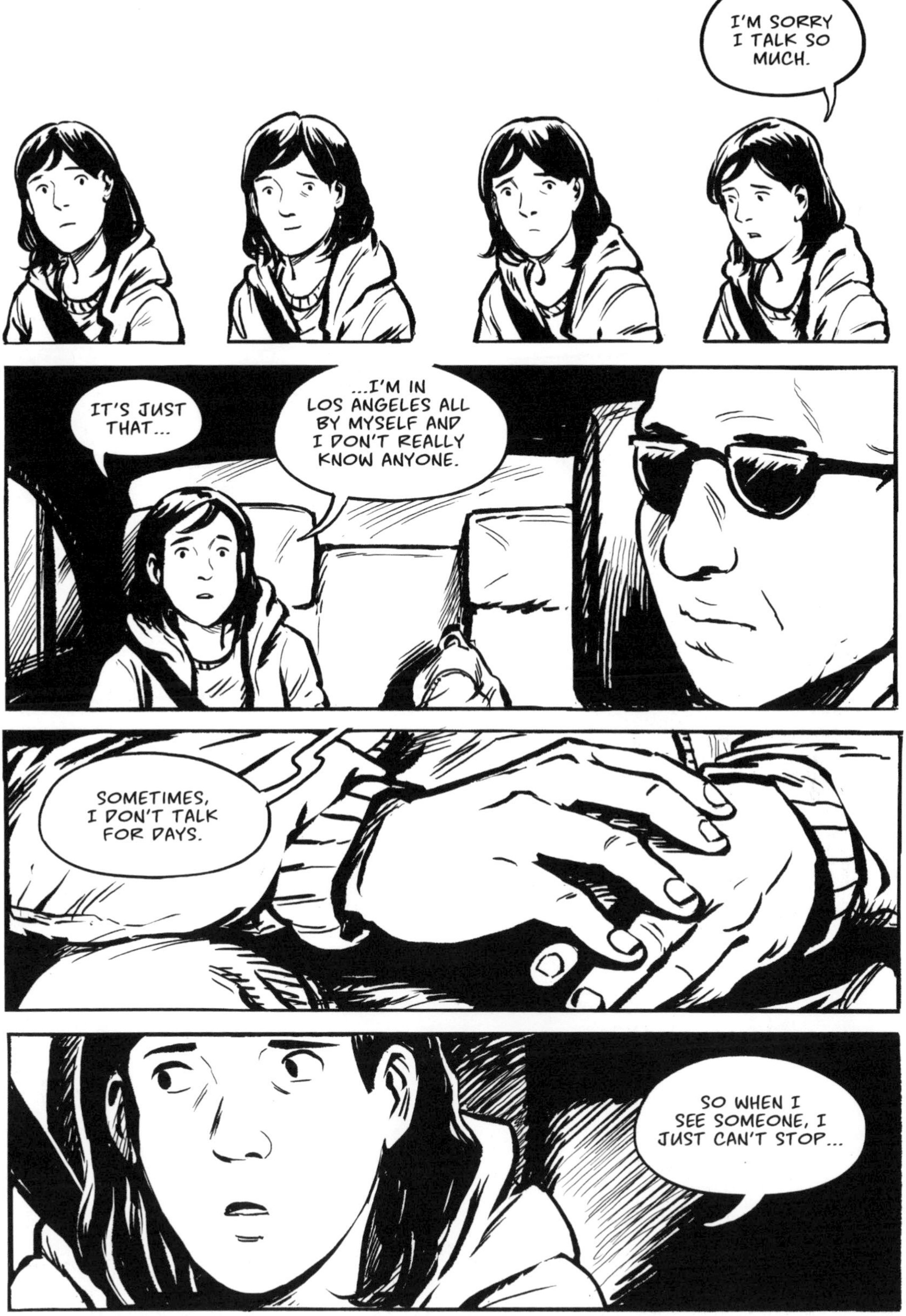
I'M SORRY I TALK SO MUCH.
IT'S JUST THAT...
...I'M IN LOS ANGELES ALL BY MYSELF AND I DON'T REALLY KNOW ANYONE.
SOMETIMES, I DON'T TALK FOR DAYS.
SO WHEN I SEE SOMEONE, I JUST CAN'T STOP...

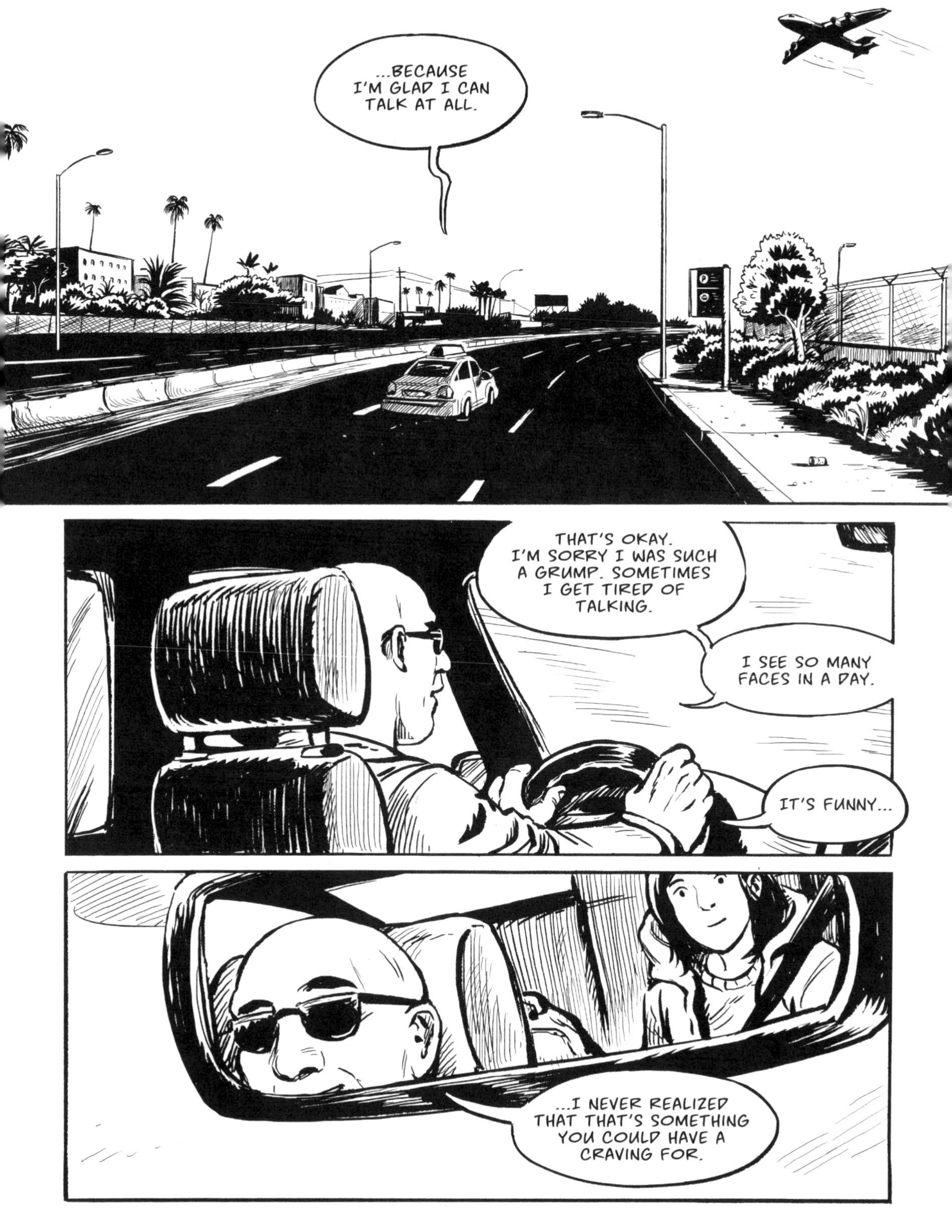
...BECAUSE I'M GLAD I CAN TALK AT ALL.
THAT'S OKAY. I'M SORRY I WAS SUCH A GRUMP. SOMETIMES I GET TIRED OF TALKING.
I SEE SO MANY FACES IN A DAY.
IT'S FUNNY...
...I NEVER REALIZED THAT THAT'S SOMETHING YOU COULD HAVE A CRAVING FOR.

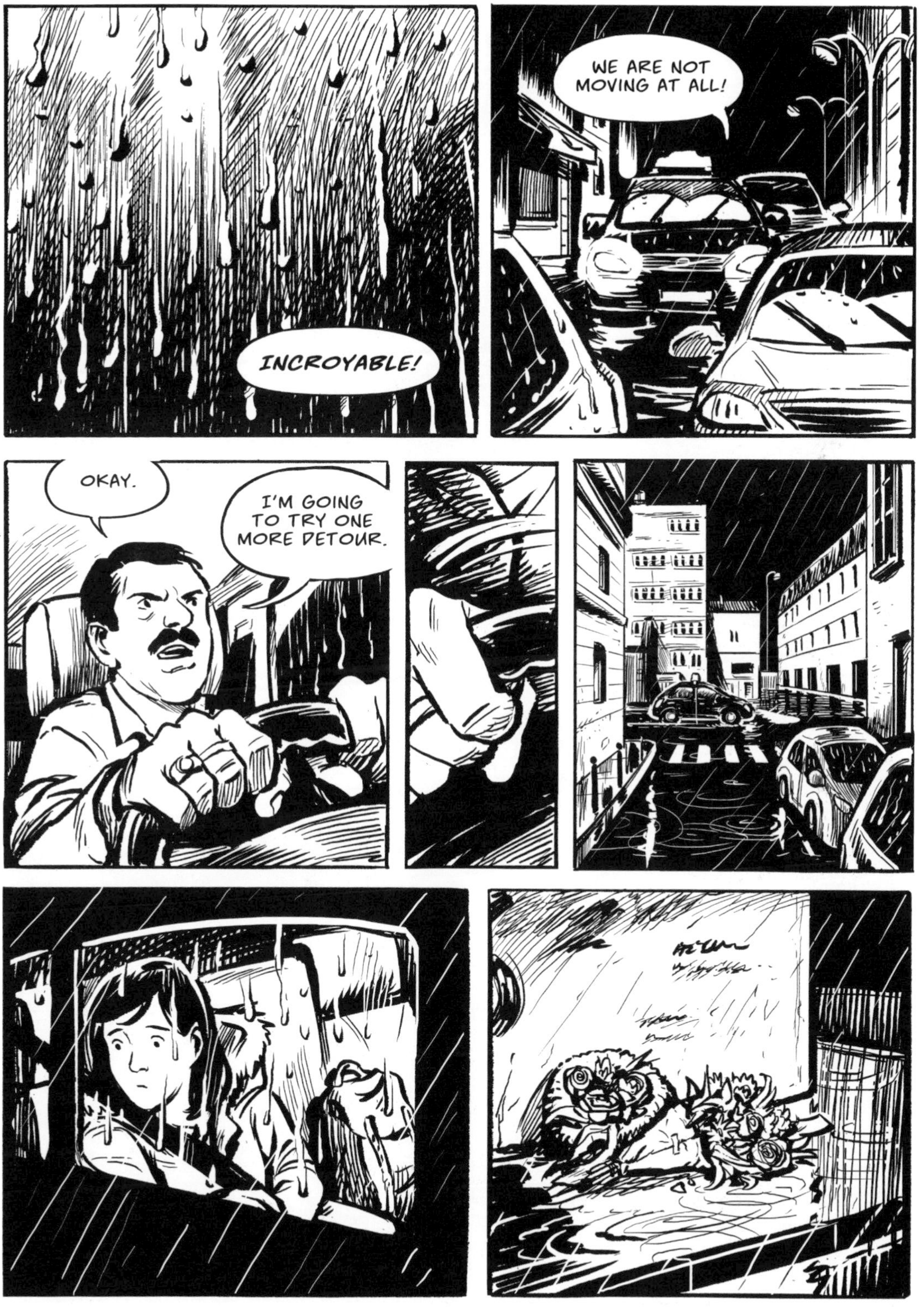
INCROYABLE!
WE ARE NOT MOVING AT ALL!
OKAY.
I'M GOING TO TRY ONE MORE DETOUR.

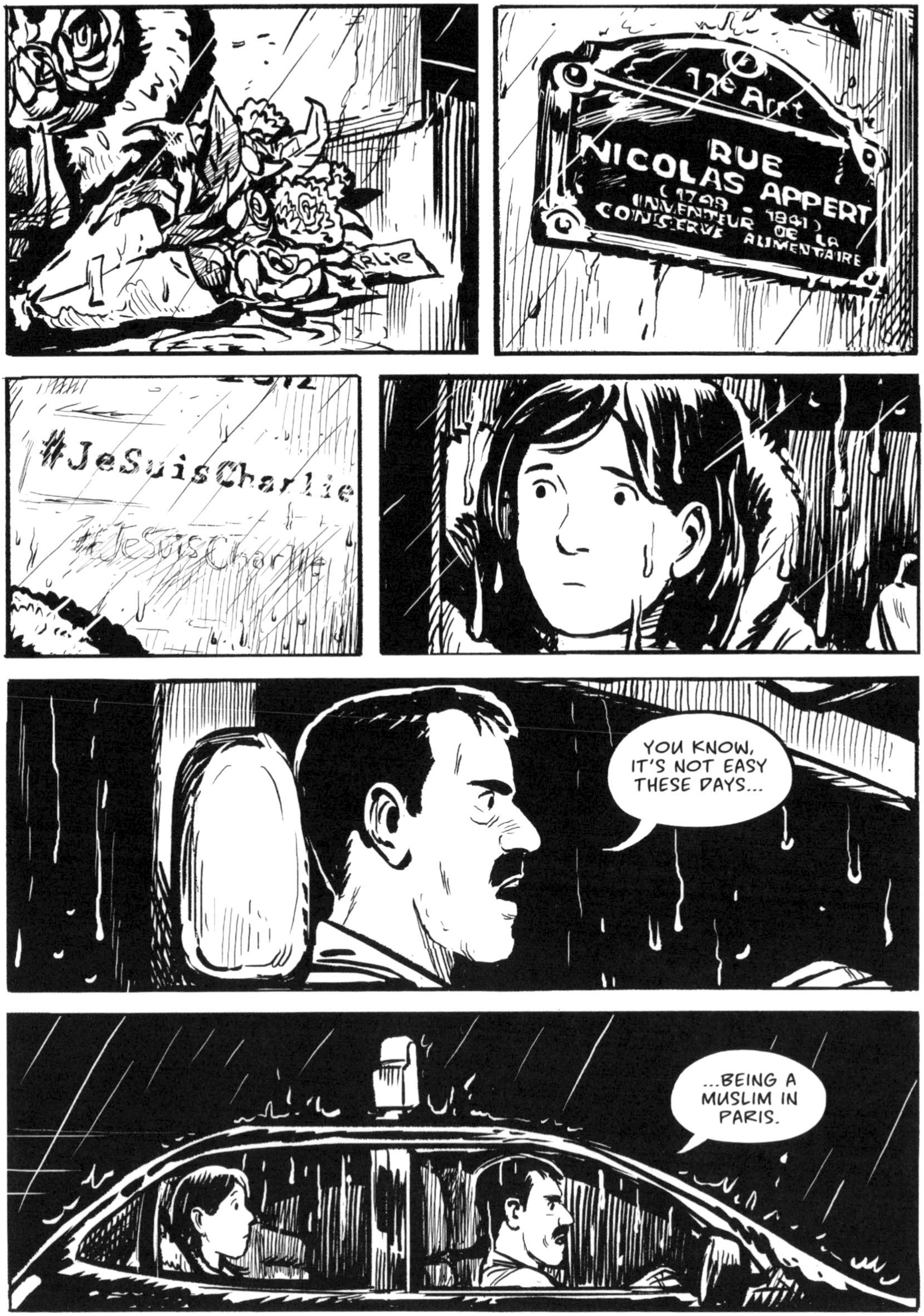
11e Arrt
RUE
NICOLAS APPERT
(1749 - 1841)
INVENTEUR DE LA
CONSERVE ALIMENTAIRE
#JeSuisCharlie
#JeSuisCharlie
YOU KNOW, IT'S NOT EASY THESE DAYS...
...BEING A MUSLIM IN PARIS.

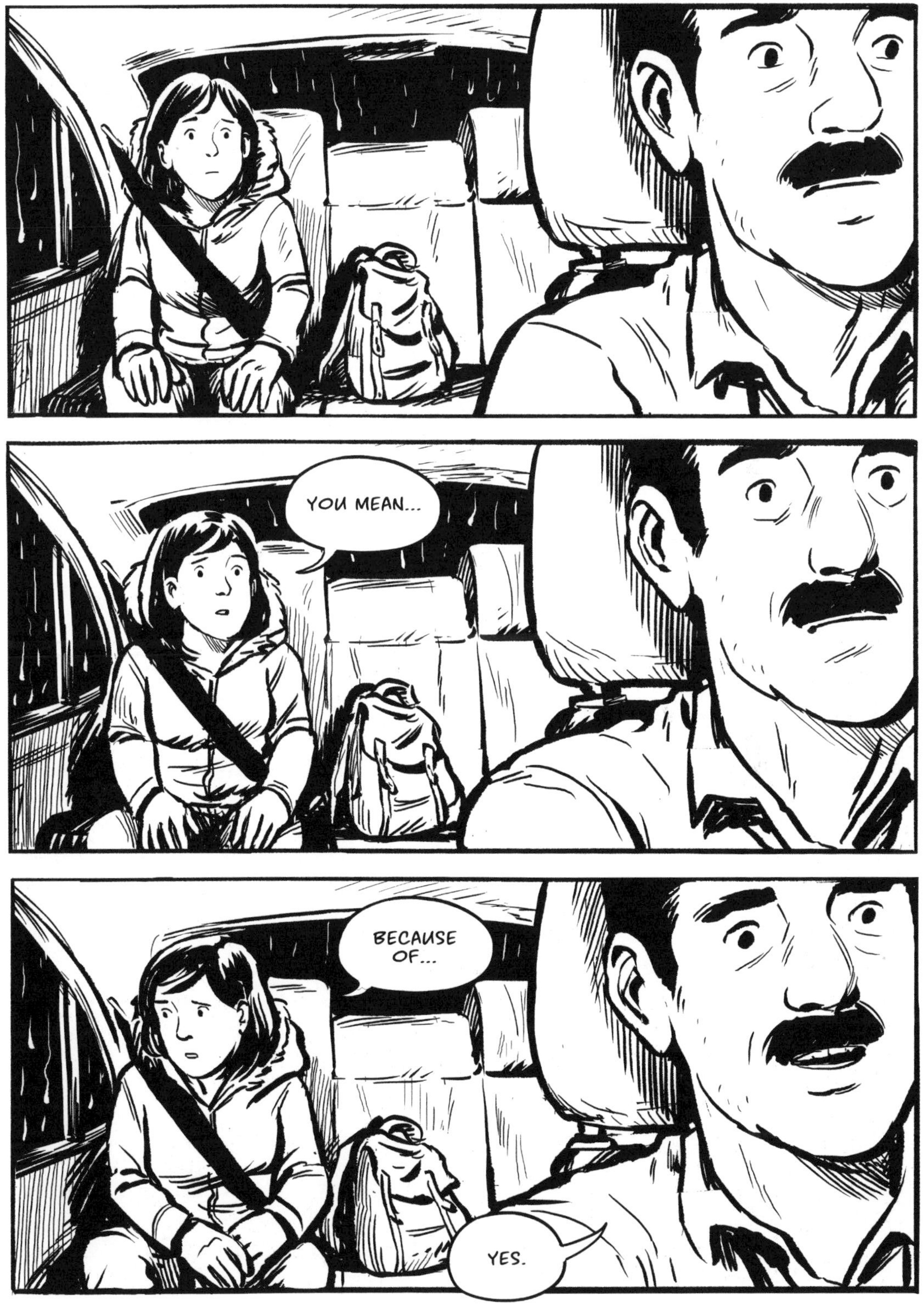
YOU MEAN...
BECAUSE OF...
YES.

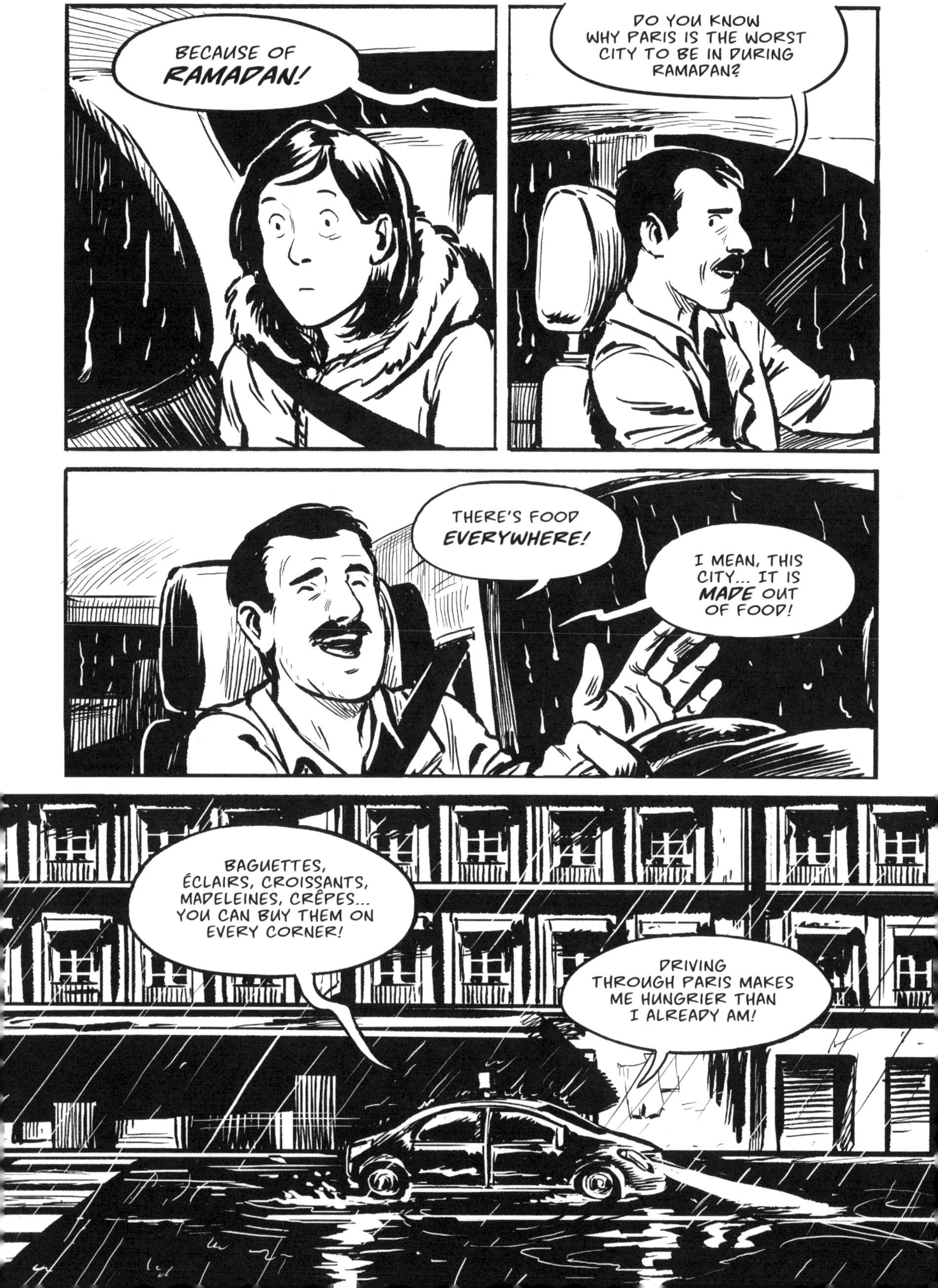
BECAUSE OF RAMADAN!
DO YOU KNOW WHY PARIS IS THE WORST CITY TO BE IN DURING RAMADAN?
THERE'S FOOD EVERYWHERE!
I MEAN, THIS CITY... IT IS MADE OUT OF FOOD!
BAGUETTES, ÉCLAIRS, CROISSANTS, MADELEINES, CRÊPES... YOU CAN BUY THEM ON EVERY CORNER!
DRIVING THROUGH PARIS MAKES ME HUNGRIER THAN I ALREADY AM!

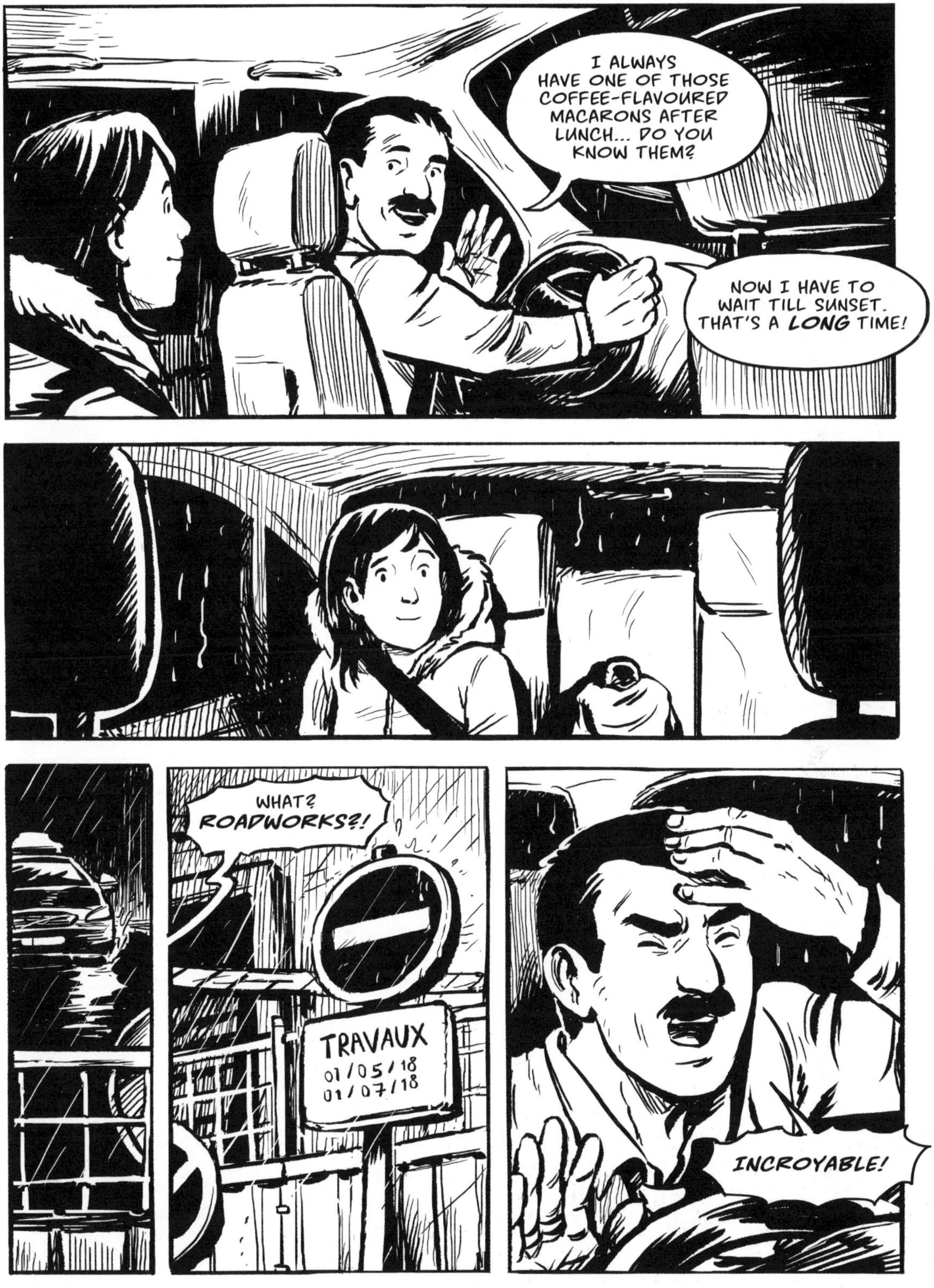
I ALWAYS HAVE ONE OF THOSE COFFEE-FLAVOURED MACARONS AFTER LUNCH... DO YOU KNOW THEM?
NOW I HAVE TO WAIT TILL SUNSET. THAT'S A **LONG** TIME!
WHAT? **ROADWORKS?!**
TRAVAUX 01/05/18 01/07/18
INCROYABLE!

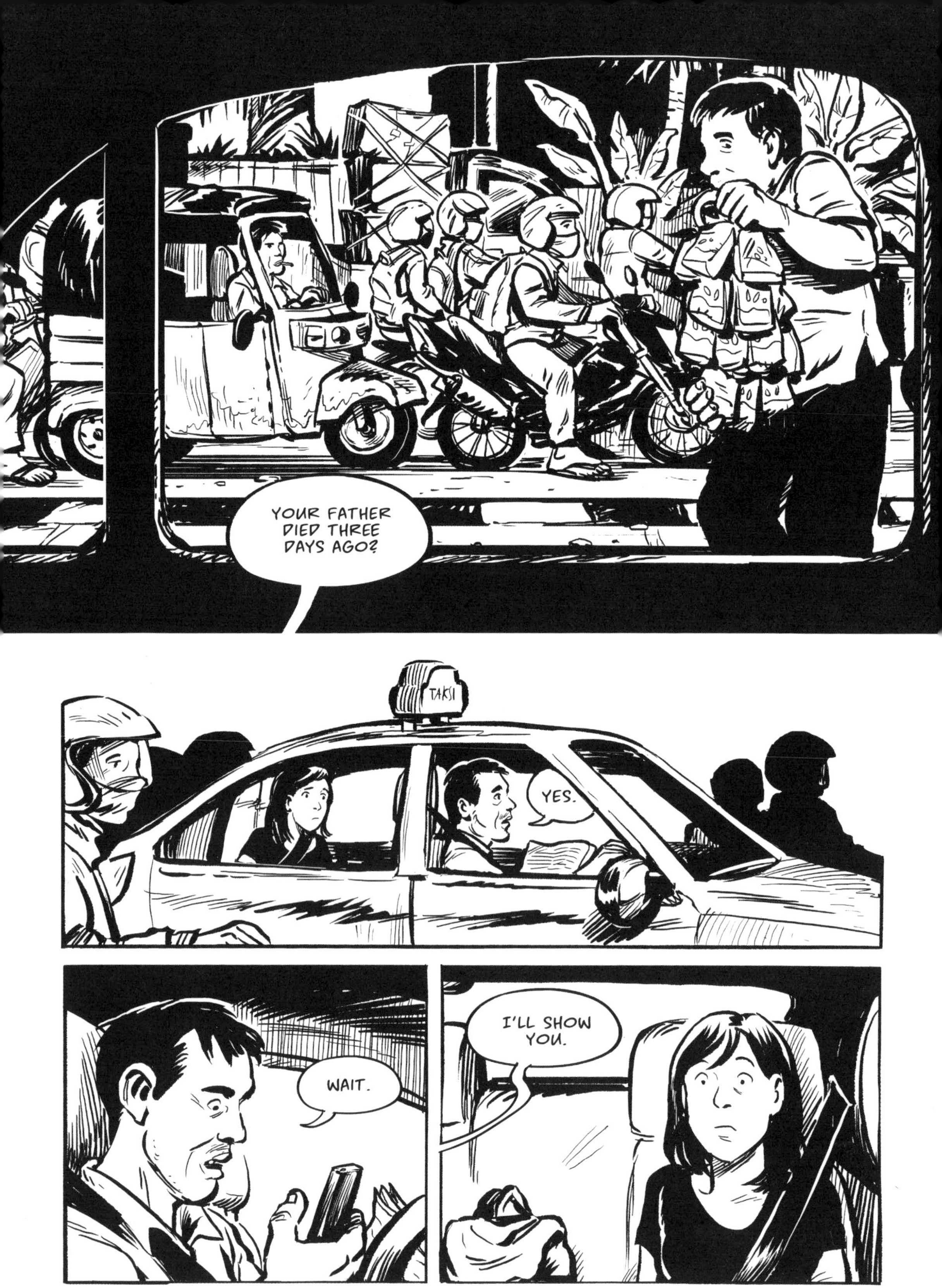
YOUR FATHER DIED THREE DAYS AGO?
TAKSI
YES.
WAIT.
I'LL SHOW YOU.

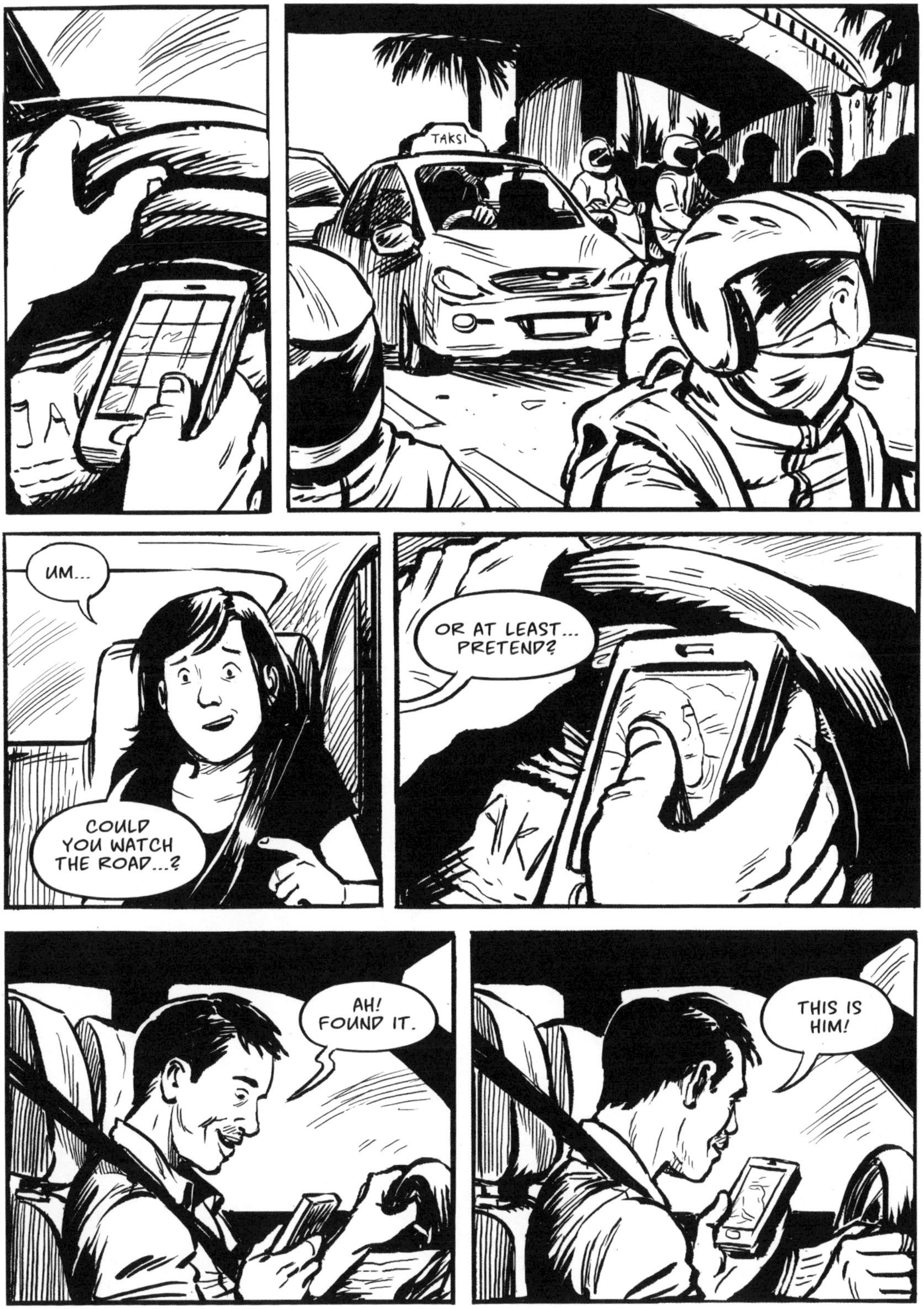
TAKSI
UM...
COULD YOU WATCH THE ROAD...?
OR AT LEAST... PRETEND?
AH! FOUND IT.
THIS IS HIM!

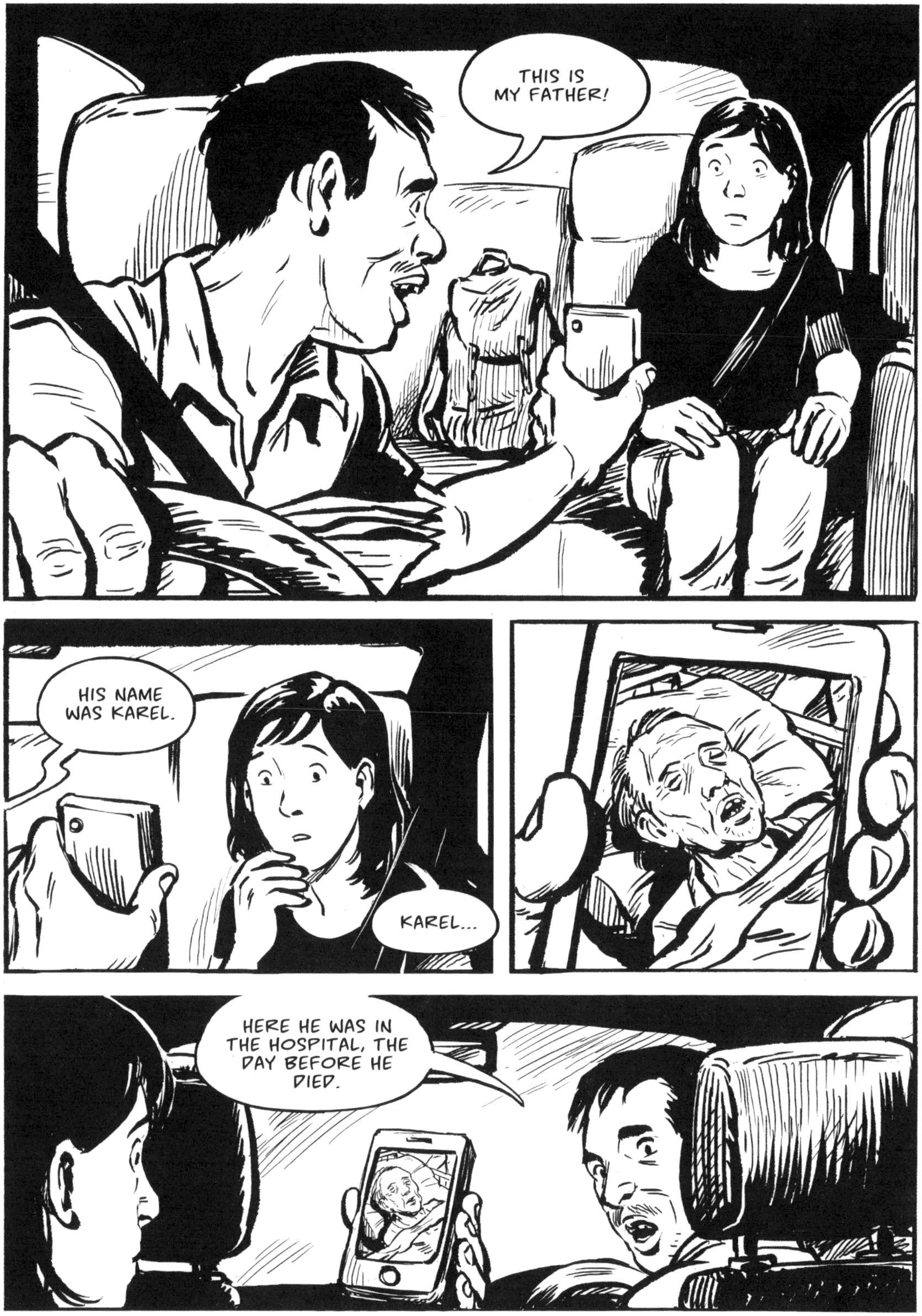
THIS IS MY FATHER!
HIS NAME WAS KAREL.
KAREL...
HERE HE WAS IN THE HOSPITAL, THE DAY BEFORE HE DIED.

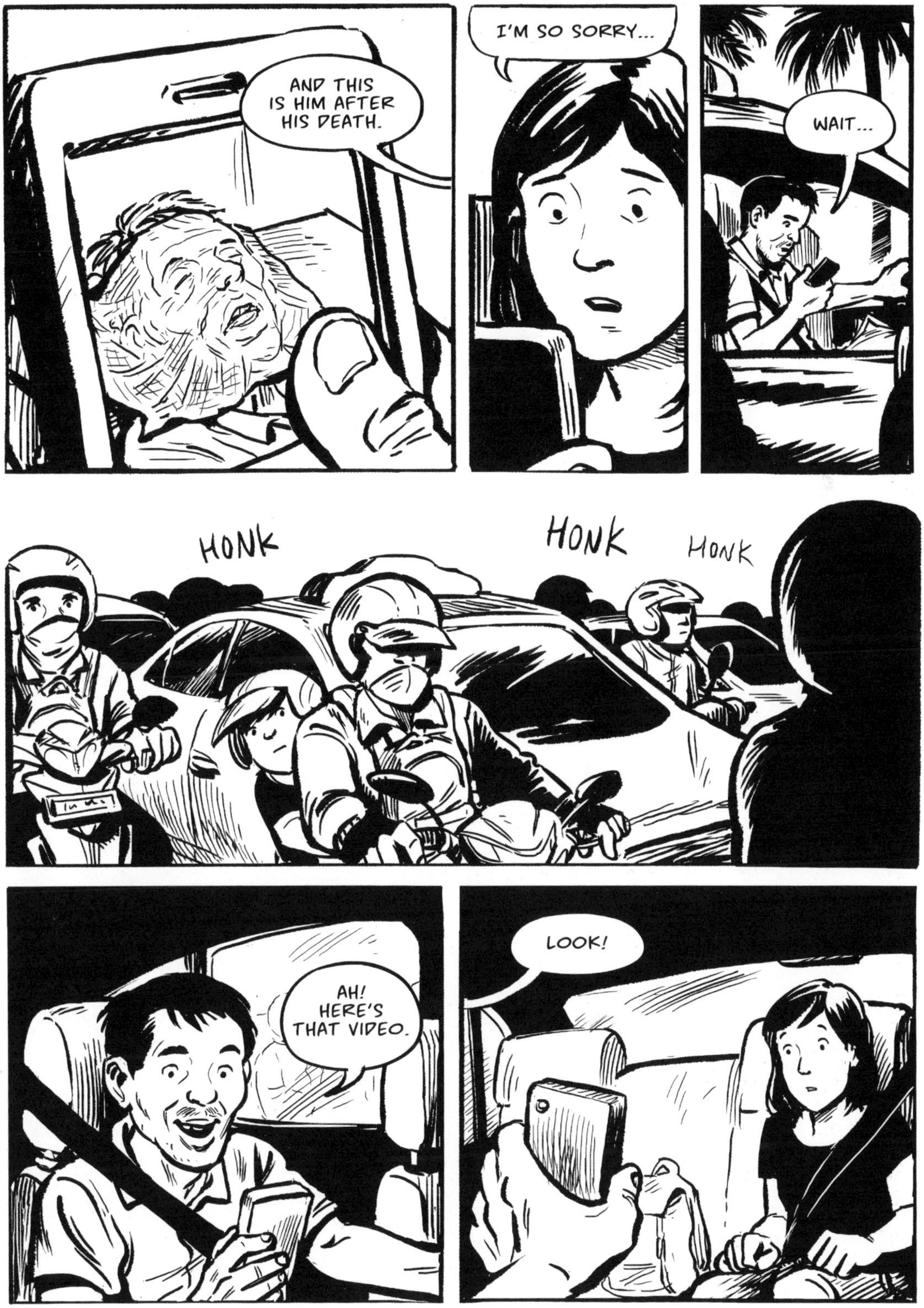
AND THIS IS HIM AFTER HIS DEATH.
I'M SO SORRY...
WAIT...
HONK
HONK
HONK
AH! HERE'S THAT VIDEO.
LOOK!

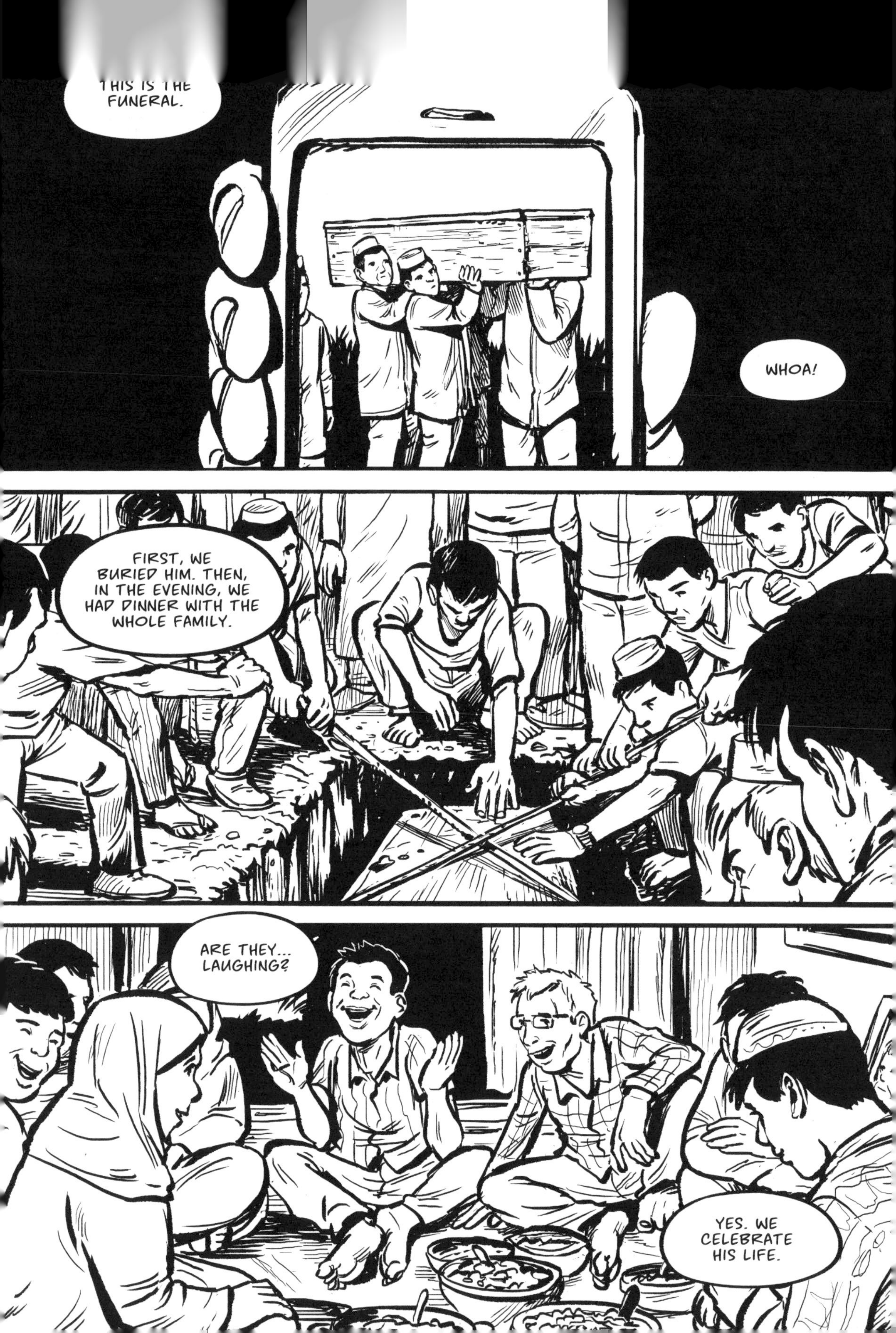

THIS IS THE FUNERAL.
WHOA!
FIRST, WE BURIED HIM. THEN, IN THE EVENING, WE HAD DINNER WITH THE WHOLE FAMILY.
ARE THEY... LAUGHING?
YES. WE CELEBRATE HIS LIFE.

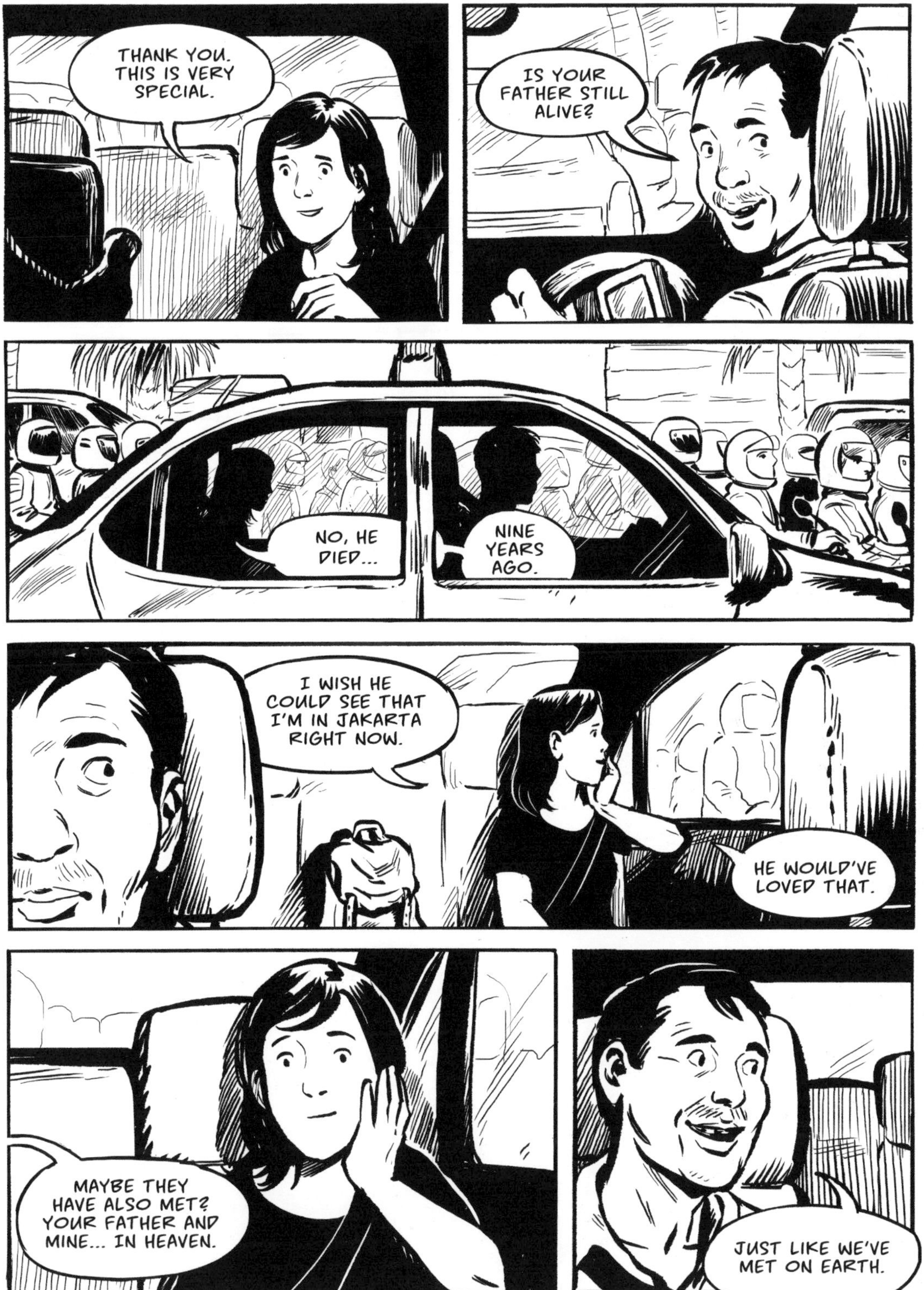
THANK YOU. THIS IS VERY SPECIAL.
IS YOUR FATHER STILL ALIVE?
NO, HE DIED...
NINE YEARS AGO.
I WISH HE COULD SEE THAT I'M IN JAKARTA RIGHT NOW.
HE WOULD'VE LOVED THAT.
MAYBE THEY HAVE ALSO MET? YOUR FATHER AND MINE... IN HEAVEN.
JUST LIKE WE'VE MET ON EARTH.

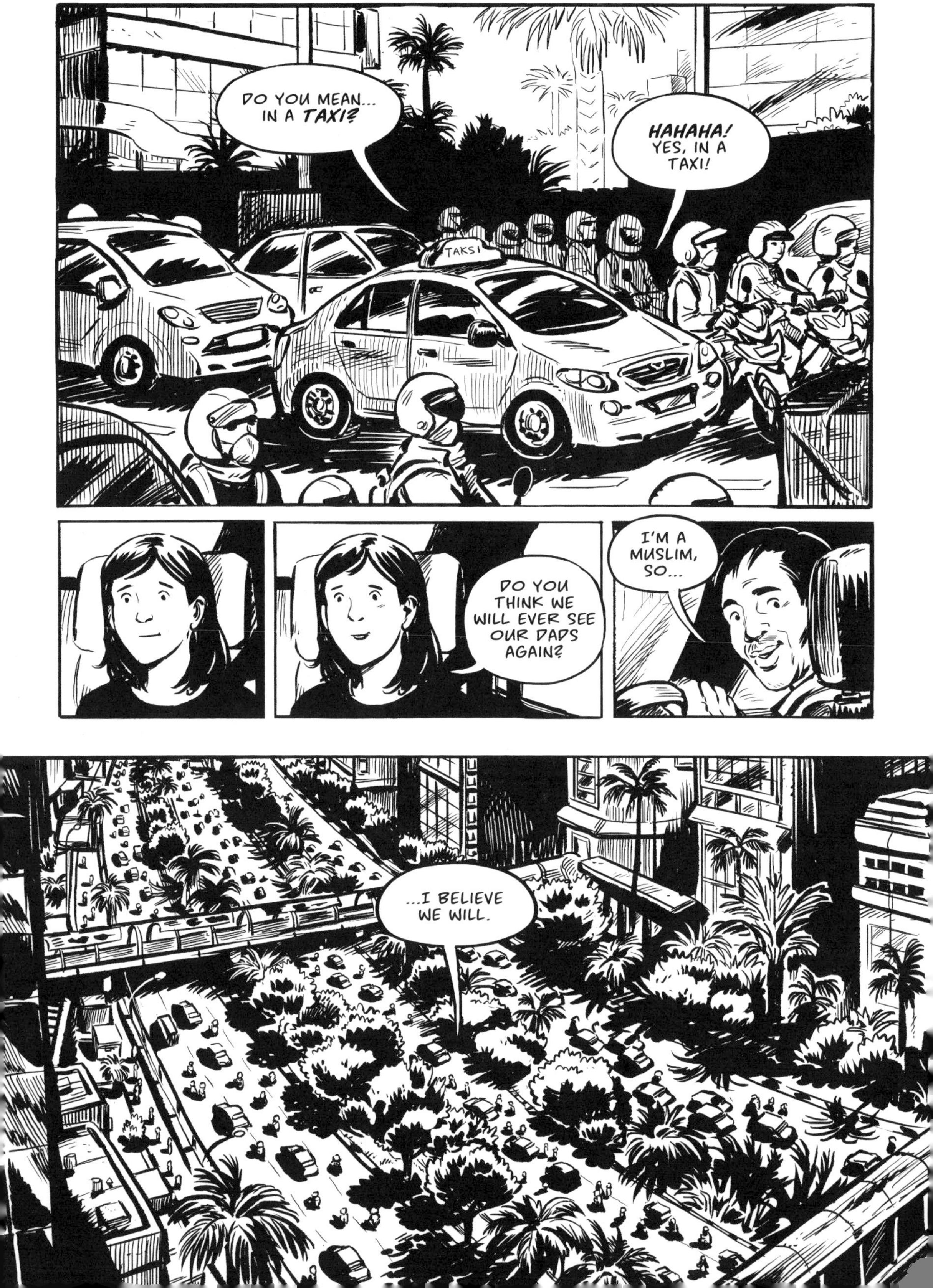
DO YOU MEAN... IN A *TAXI?*
HAHAHA! YES, IN A TAXI!
TAKSI
DO YOU THINK WE WILL EVER SEE OUR DADS AGAIN?
I'M A MUSLIM, SO...
...I BELIEVE WE WILL.

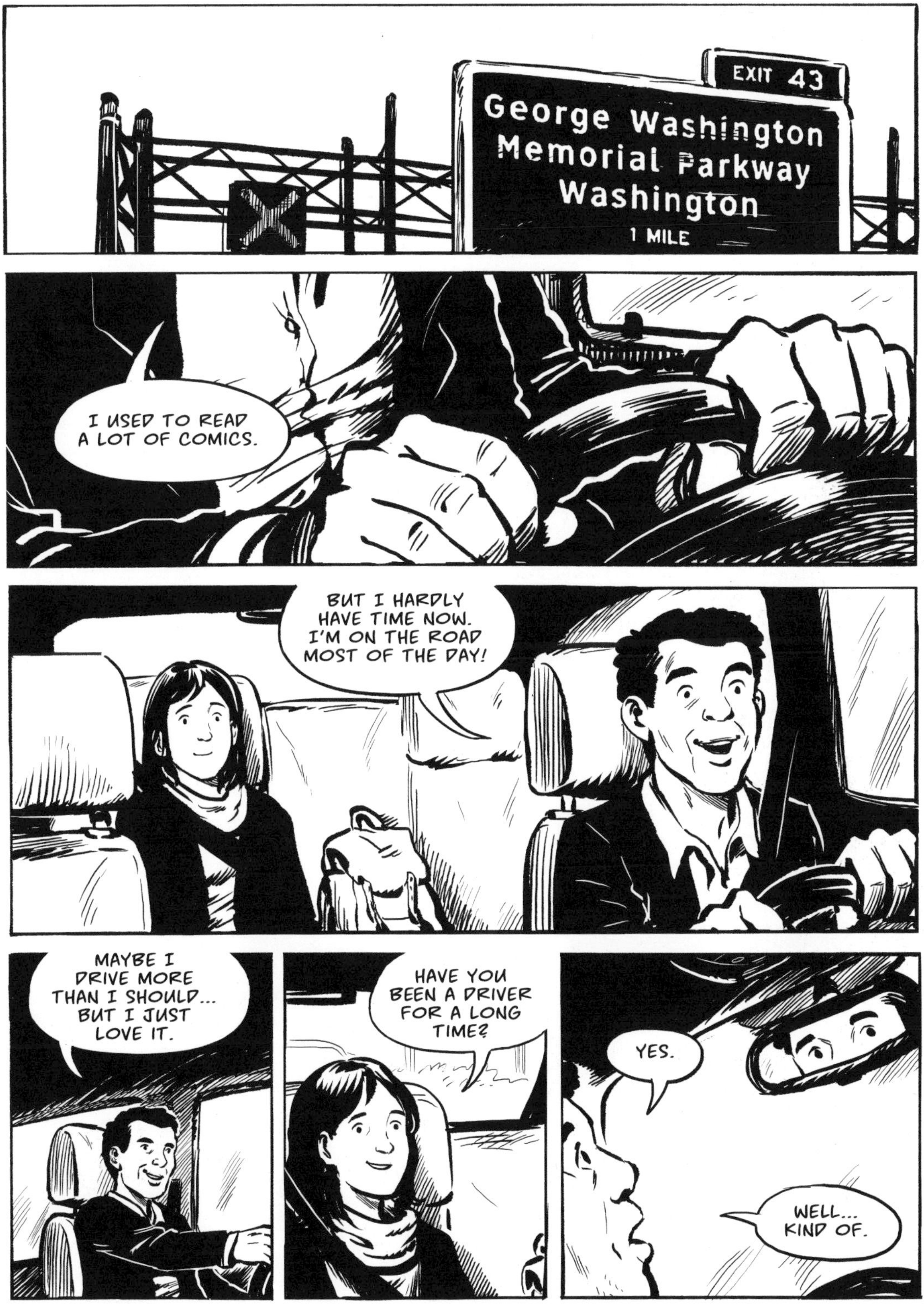
EXIT 43
George Washington
Memorial Parkway
Washington
1 MILE
I USED TO READ A LOT OF COMICS.
BUT I HARDLY HAVE TIME NOW. I'M ON THE ROAD MOST OF THE DAY!
MAYBE I DRIVE MORE THAN I SHOULD... BUT I JUST LOVE IT.
HAVE YOU BEEN A DRIVER FOR A LONG TIME?
YES.
WELL... KIND OF.

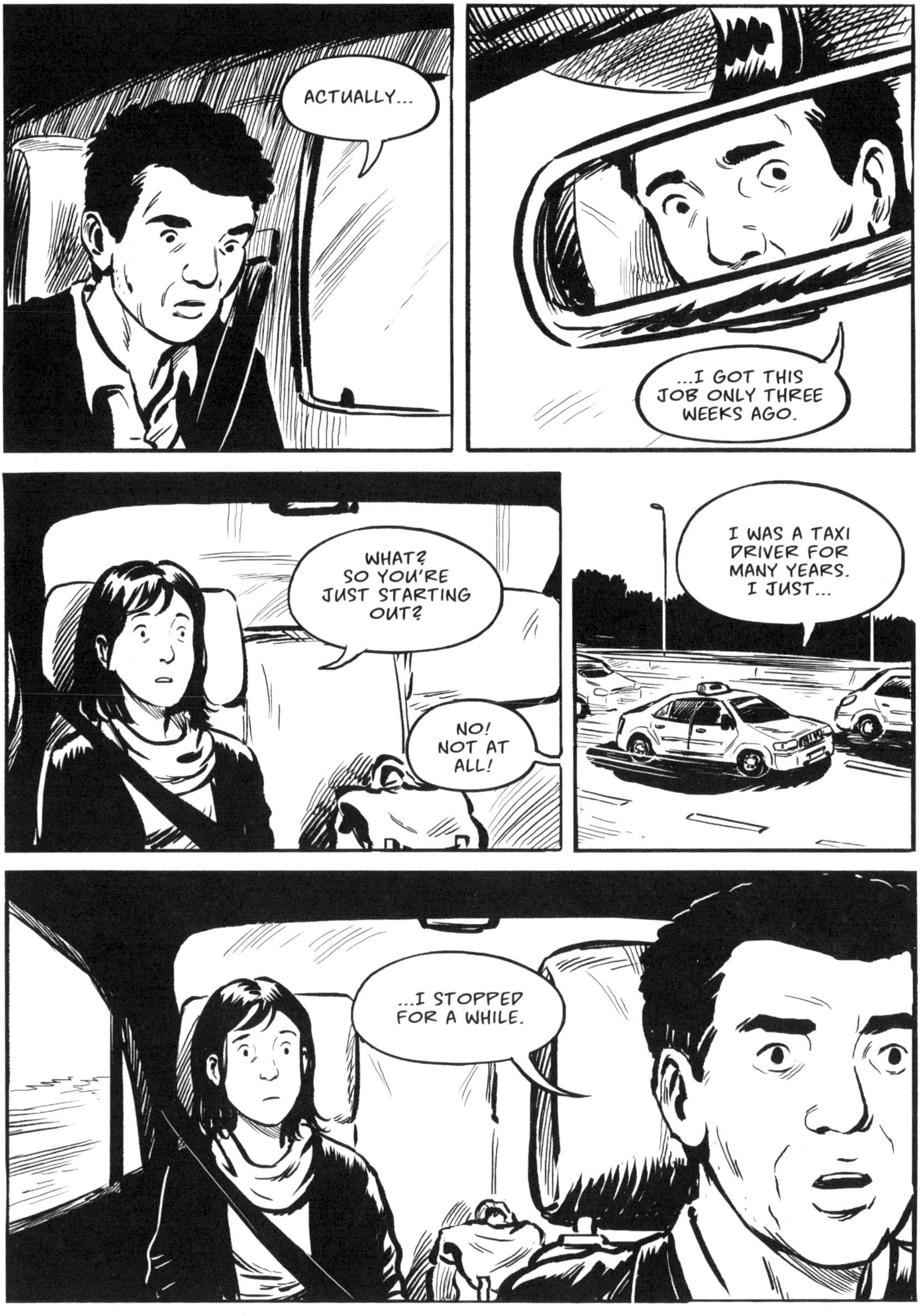
ACTUALLY...
...I GOT THIS JOB ONLY THREE WEEKS AGO.
WHAT? SO YOU'RE JUST STARTING OUT?
NO! NOT AT ALL!
I WAS A TAXI DRIVER FOR MANY YEARS. I JUST...
...I STOPPED FOR A WHILE.

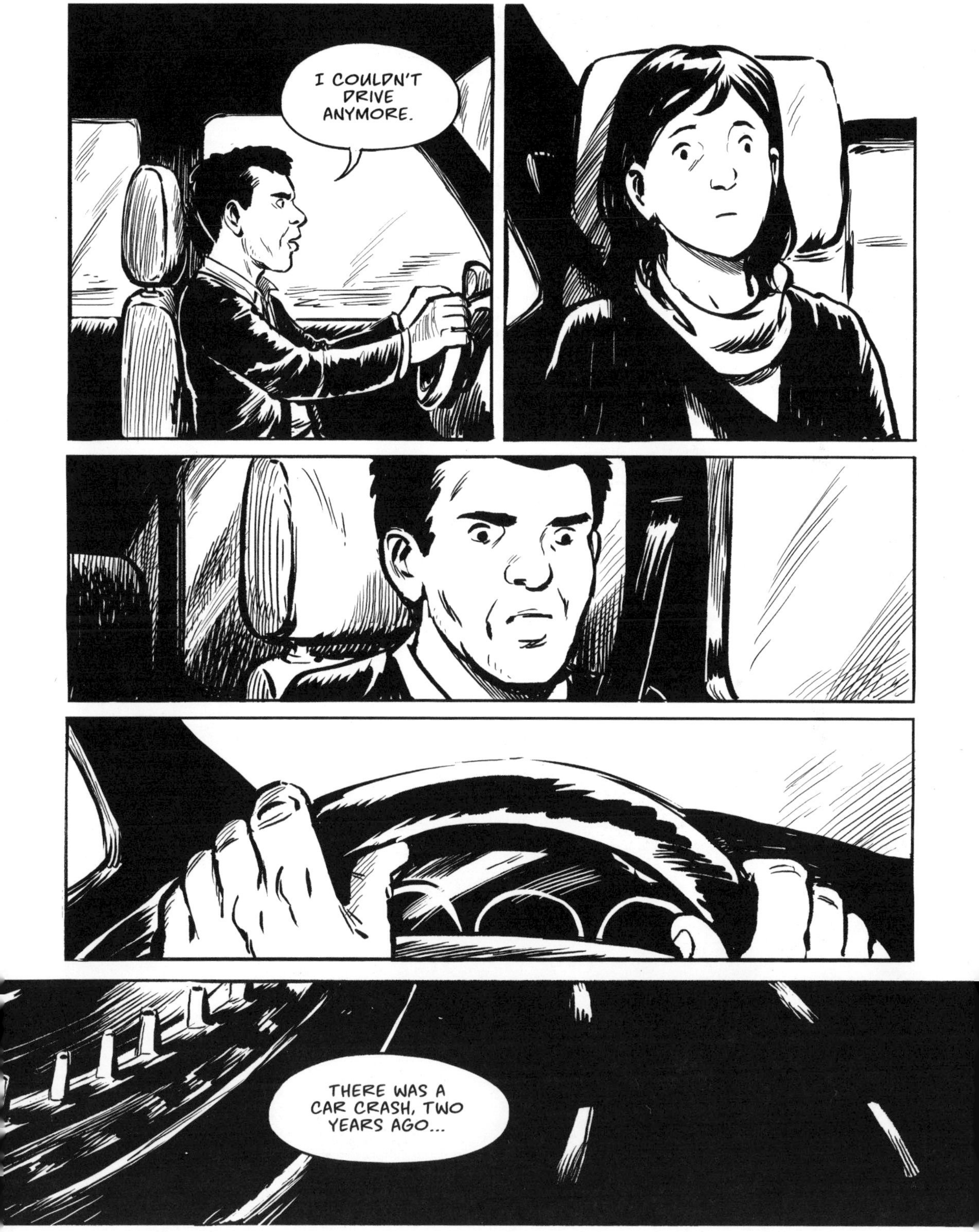
I COULDN'T DRIVE ANYMORE.
THERE WAS A CAR CRASH, TWO YEARS AGO...

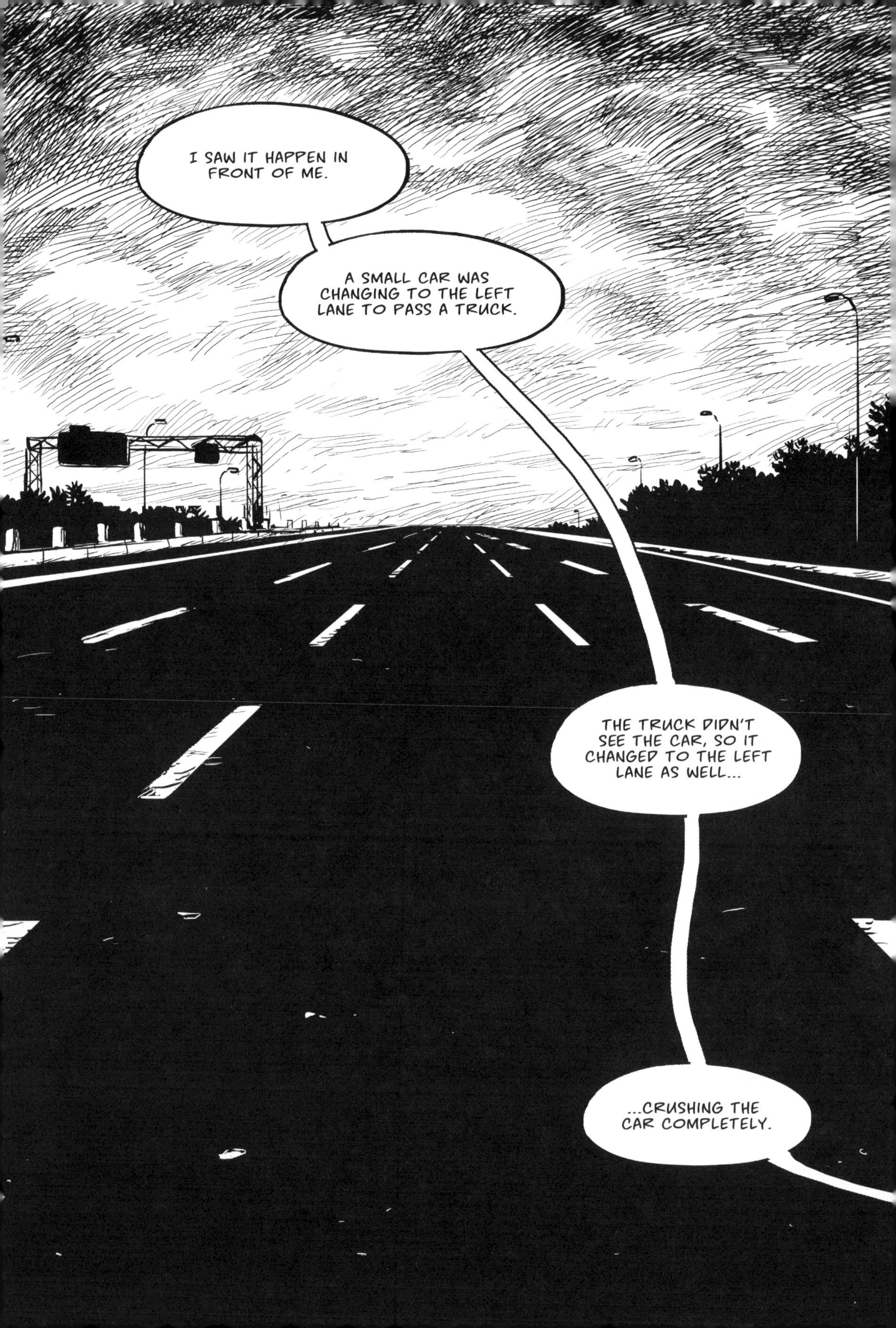
I SAW IT HAPPEN IN FRONT OF ME.
A SMALL CAR WAS CHANGING TO THE LEFT LANE TO PASS A TRUCK.
THE TRUCK DIDN'T SEE THE CAR, SO IT CHANGED TO THE LEFT LANE AS WELL...
...CRUSHING THE CAR COMPLETELY.

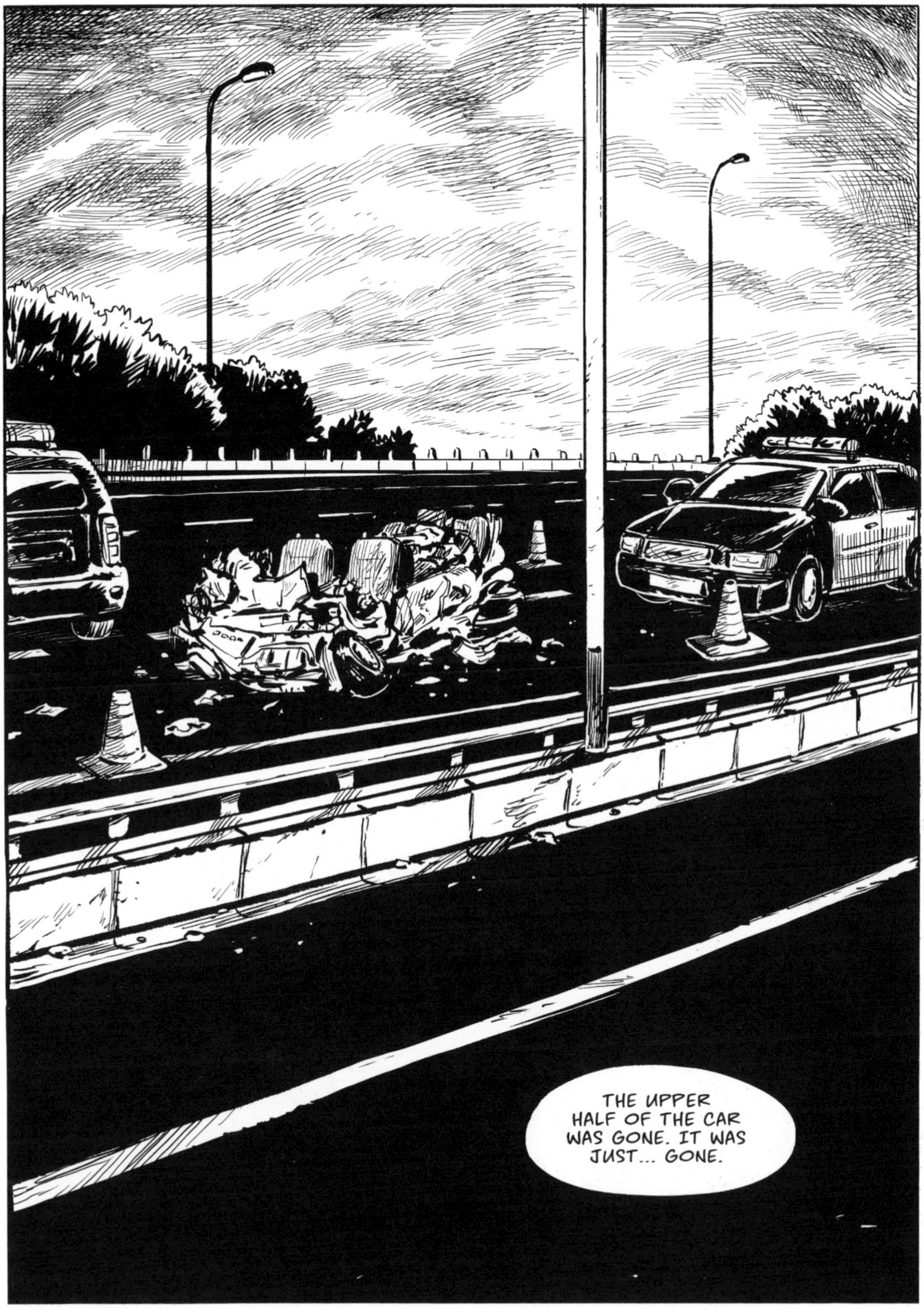
THE UPPER HALF OF THE CAR WAS GONE. IT WAS JUST... GONE.

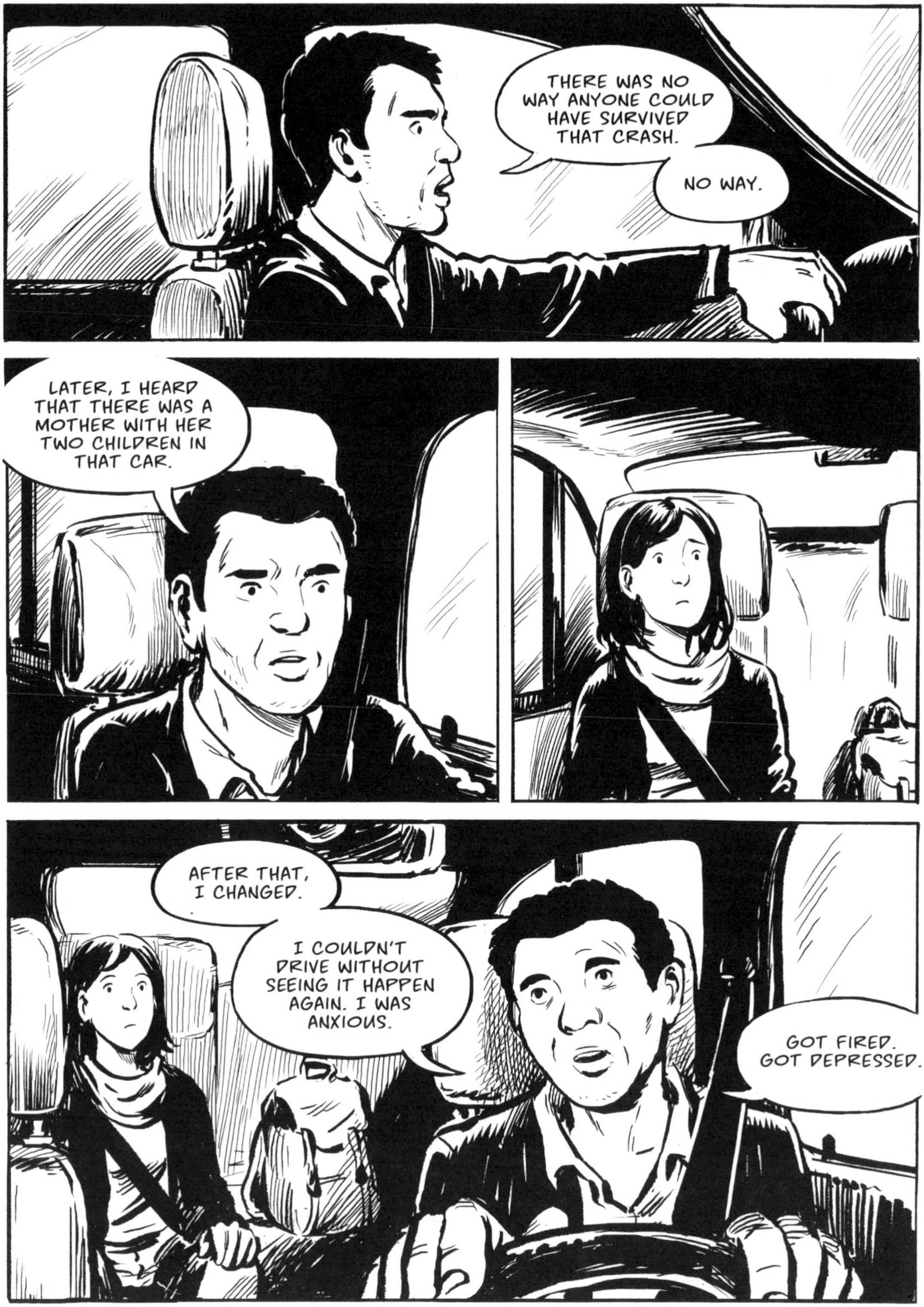
THERE WAS NO WAY ANYONE COULD HAVE SURVIVED THAT CRASH.
NO WAY.
LATER, I HEARD THAT THERE WAS A MOTHER WITH HER TWO CHILDREN IN THAT CAR.
AFTER THAT, I CHANGED.
I COULDN'T DRIVE WITHOUT SEEING IT HAPPEN AGAIN. I WAS ANXIOUS.
GOT FIRED. GOT DEPRESSED.

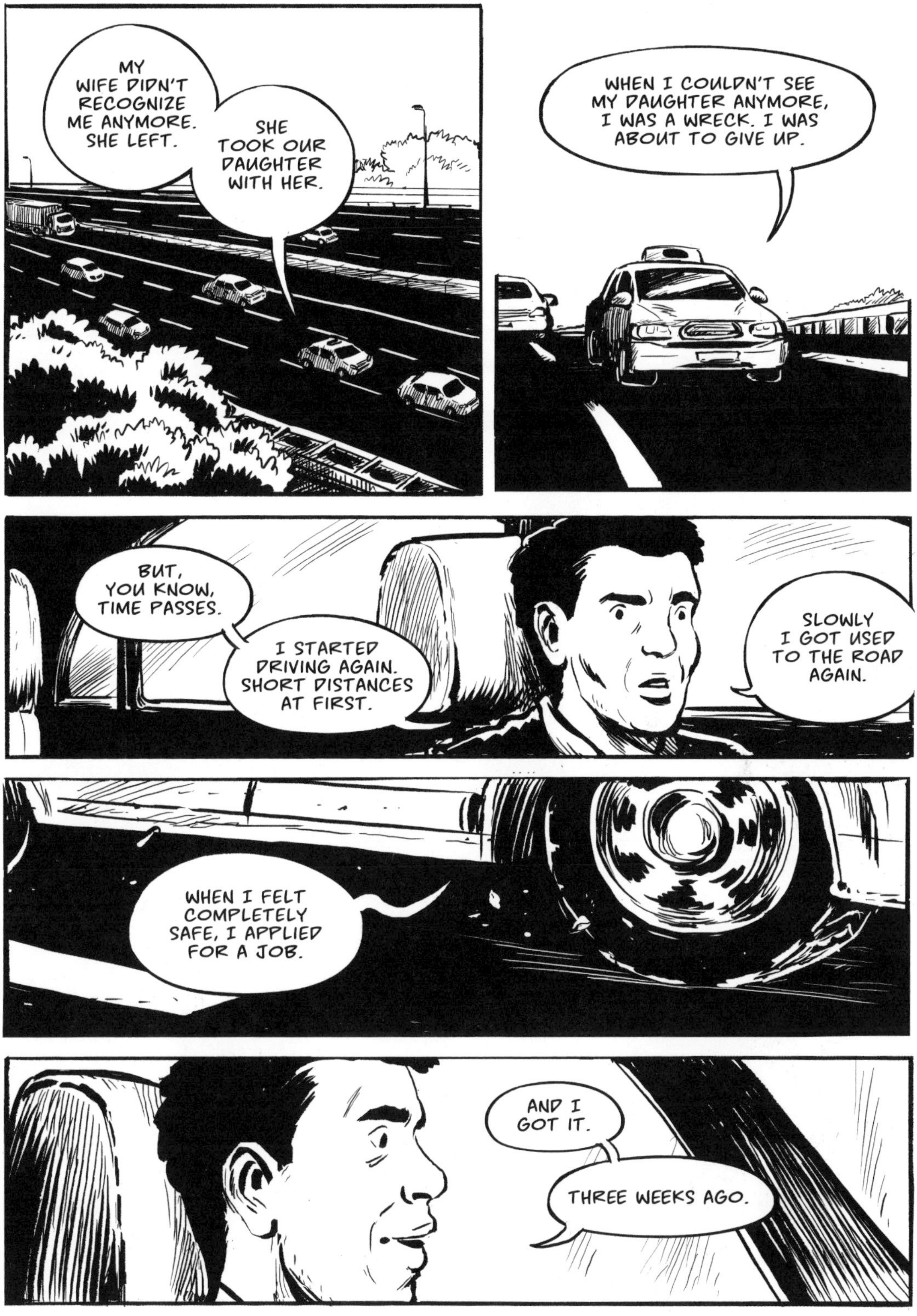
MY WIFE DIDN'T RECOGNIZE ME ANYMORE. SHE LEFT.
SHE TOOK OUR DAUGHTER WITH HER.
WHEN I COULDN'T SEE MY DAUGHTER ANYMORE, I WAS A WRECK. I WAS ABOUT TO GIVE UP.
BUT, YOU KNOW, TIME PASSES.
I STARTED DRIVING AGAIN. SHORT DISTANCES AT FIRST.
SLOWLY I GOT USED TO THE ROAD AGAIN.
WHEN I FELT COMPLETELY SAFE, I APPLIED FOR A JOB.
AND I GOT IT.
THREE WEEKS AGO.

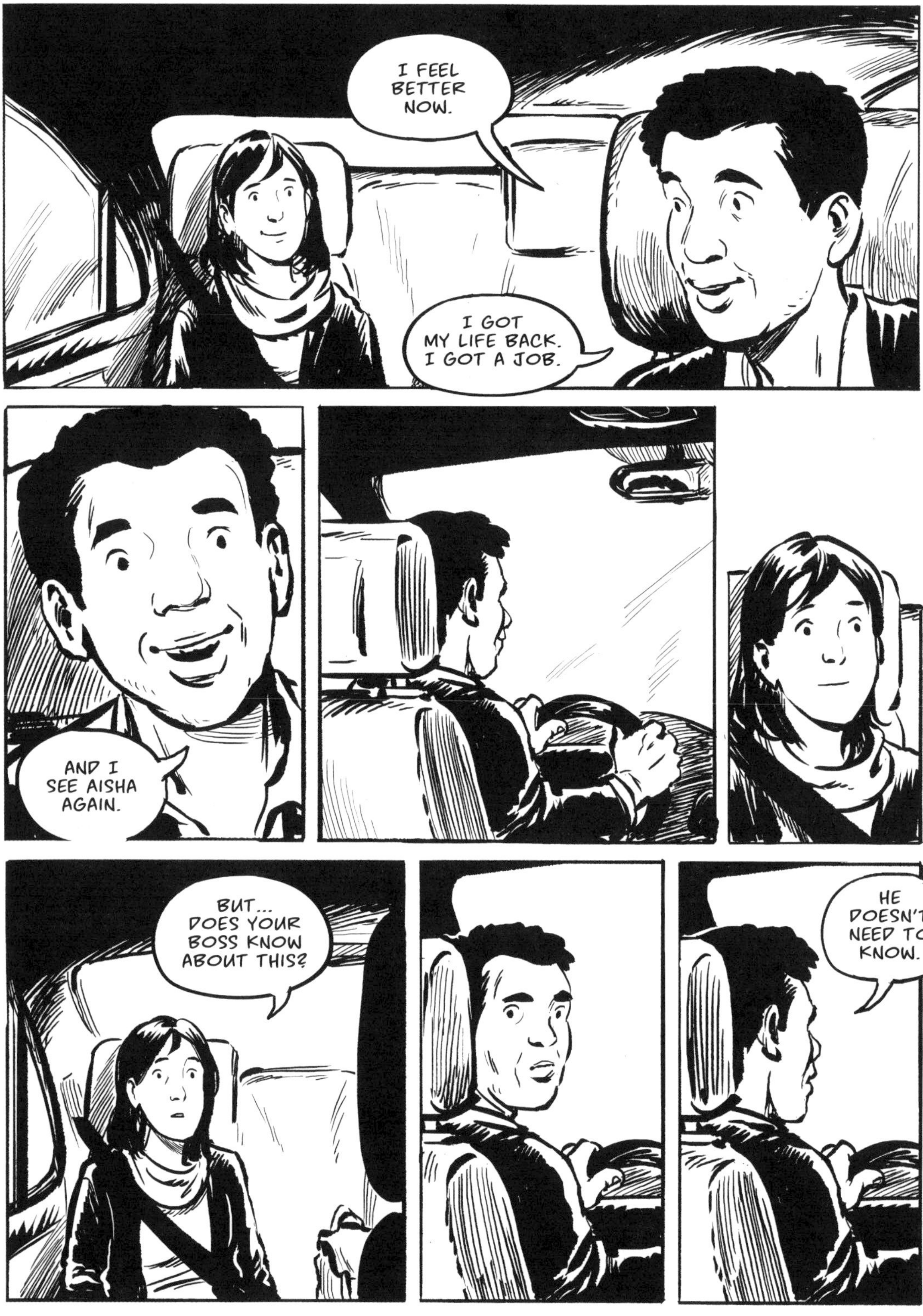
I FEEL BETTER NOW.
I GOT MY LIFE BACK. I GOT A JOB.
AND I SEE AISHA AGAIN.
BUT... DOES YOUR BOSS KNOW ABOUT THIS?
HE DOESN'T NEED TO KNOW.

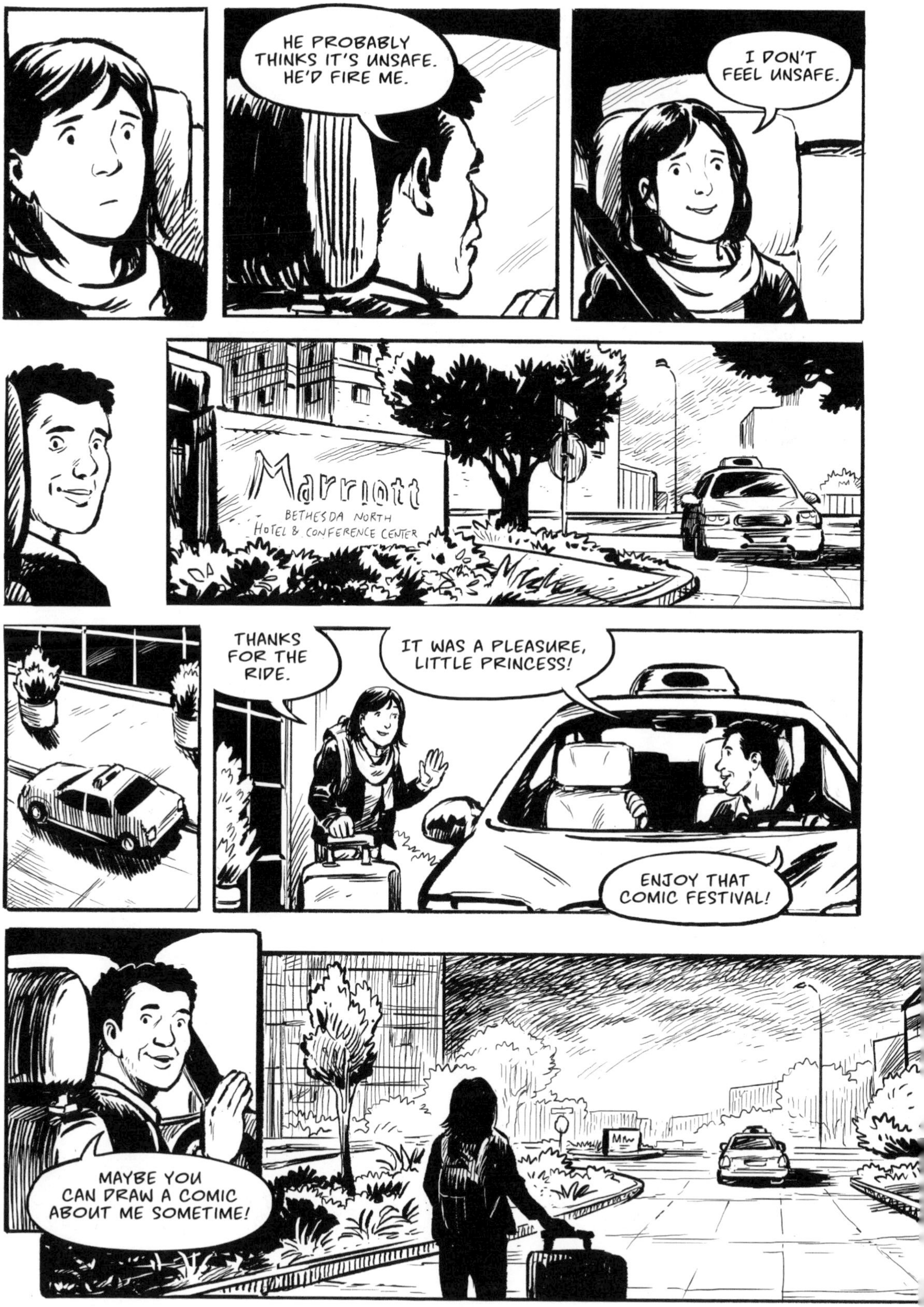
HE PROBABLY THINKS IT'S UNSAFE. HE'D FIRE ME.
I DON'T FEEL UNSAFE.
Marriott
BETHESDA NORTH
HOTEL & CONFERENCE CENTER
THANKS FOR THE RIDE.
IT WAS A PLEASURE, LITTLE PRINCESS!
ENJOY THAT COMIC FESTIVAL!
MAYBE YOU CAN DRAW A COMIC ABOUT ME SOMETIME!

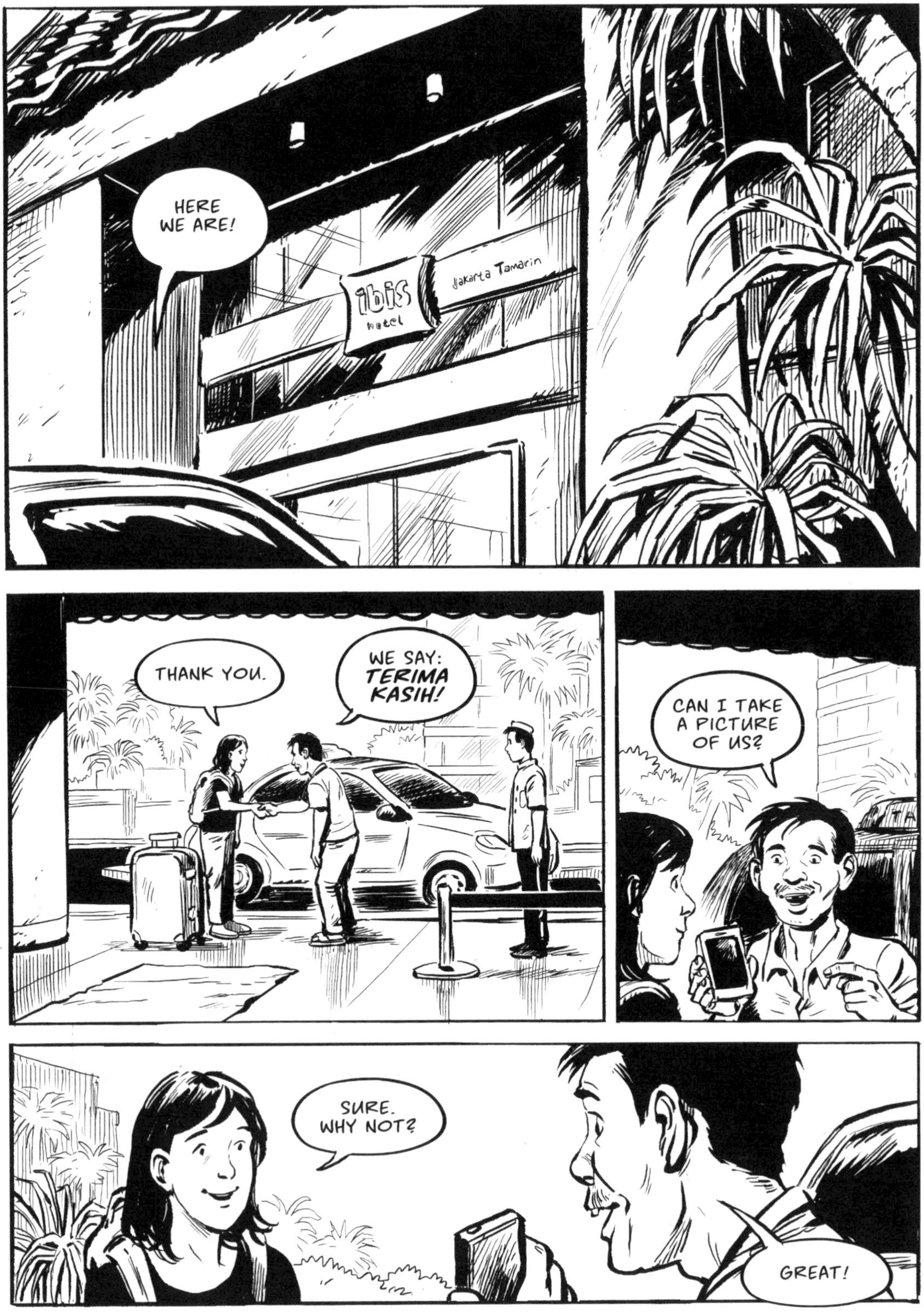
HERE WE ARE!
ibis hotel
Jakarta Tamarin
THANK YOU.
WE SAY: TERIMA KASIH!
CAN I TAKE A PICTURE OF US?
SURE. WHY NOT?
GREAT!

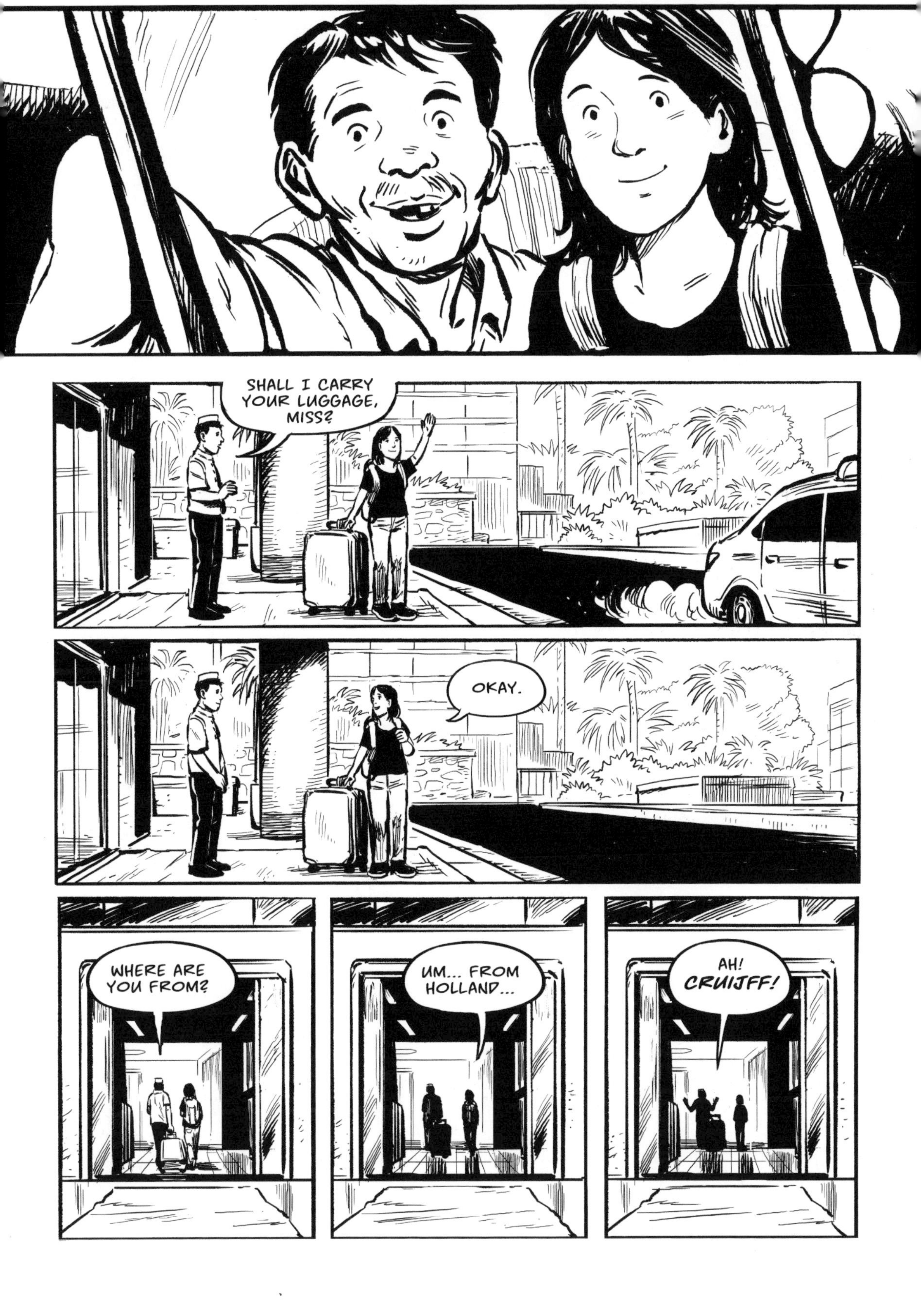
SHALL I CARRY YOUR LUGGAGE, MISS?
OKAY.
WHERE ARE YOU FROM?
UM... FROM HOLLAND...
AH! CRUIJFF!

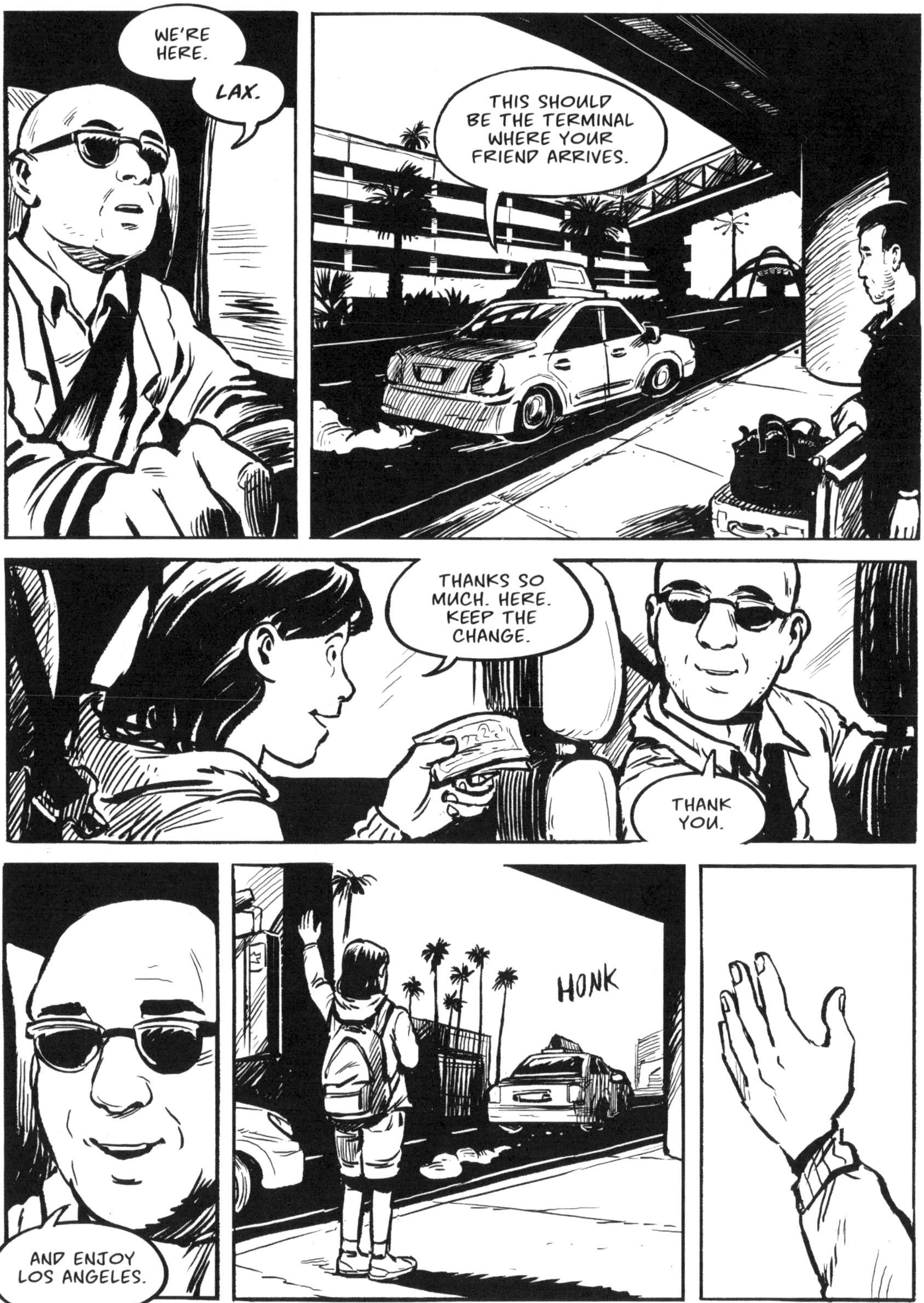
WE'RE HERE.
LAX.
THIS SHOULD BE THE TERMINAL WHERE YOUR FRIEND ARRIVES.
THANKS SO MUCH. HERE. KEEP THE CHANGE.
THANK YOU.
AND ENJOY LOS ANGELES.
HONK

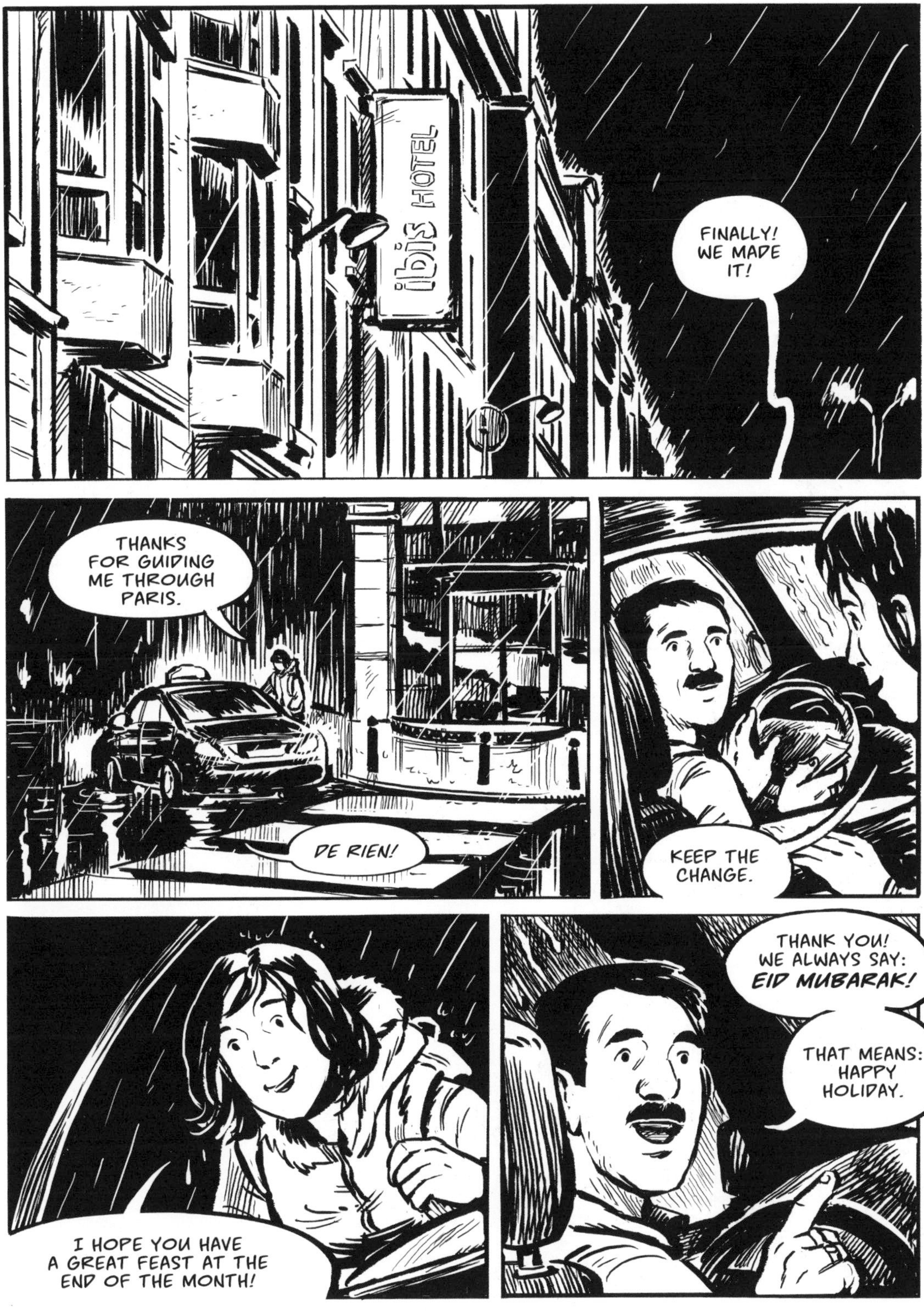
ibis HOTEL
FINALLY! WE MADE IT!
THANKS FOR GUIDING ME THROUGH PARIS.
DE RIEN!
KEEP THE CHANGE.
I HOPE YOU HAVE A GREAT FEAST AT THE END OF THE MONTH!
THANK YOU! WE ALWAYS SAY: **EID MUBARAK!**
THAT MEANS: HAPPY HOLIDAY.

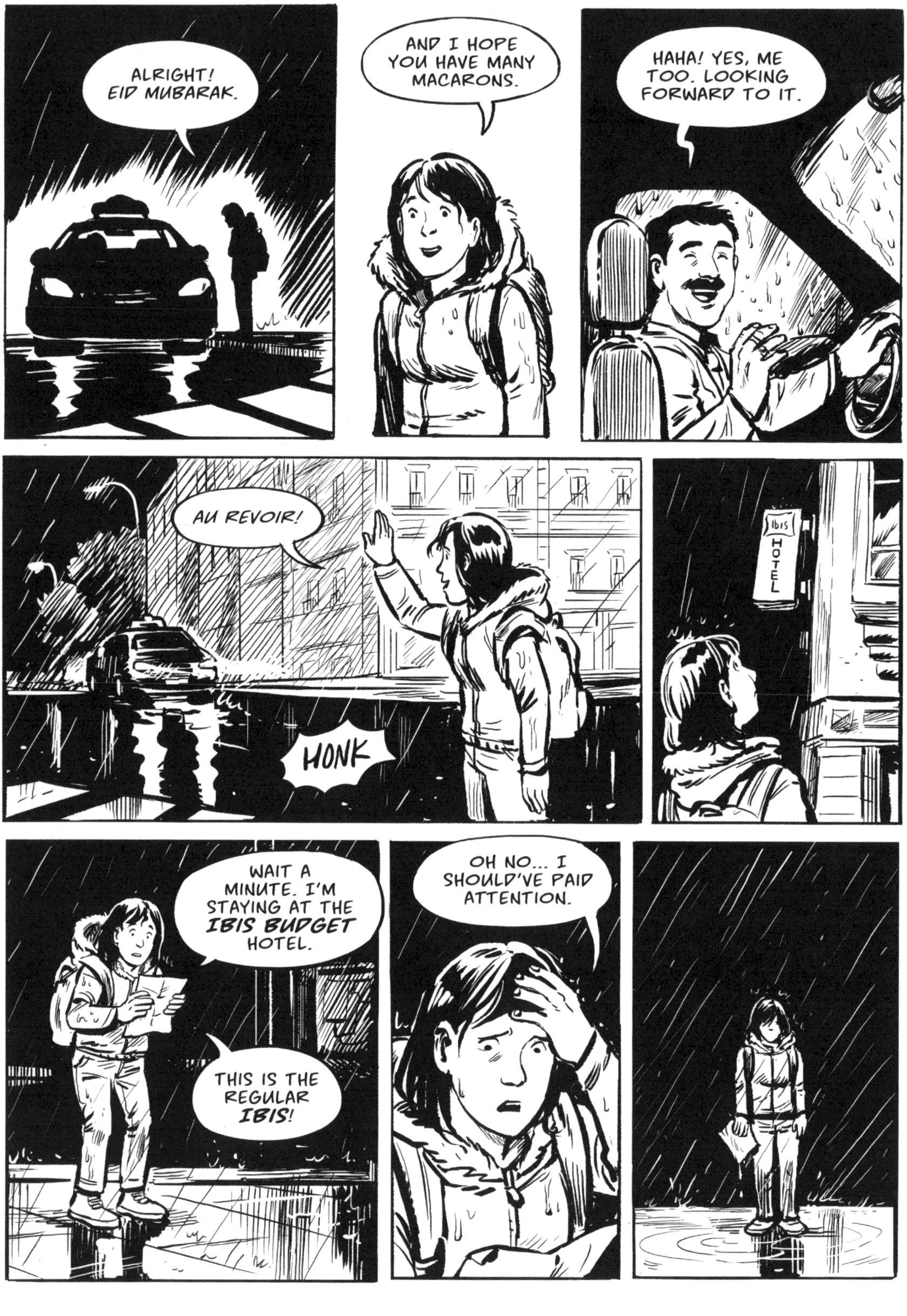
ALRIGHT! EID MUBARAK.
AND I HOPE YOU HAVE MANY MACARONS.
HAHA! YES, ME TOO. LOOKING FORWARD TO IT.
AU REVOIR!
HONK
Ibis HOTEL
WAIT A MINUTE. I'M STAYING AT THE IBIS BUDGET HOTEL.
THIS IS THE REGULAR IBIS!
OH NO... I SHOULD'VE PAID ATTENTION.

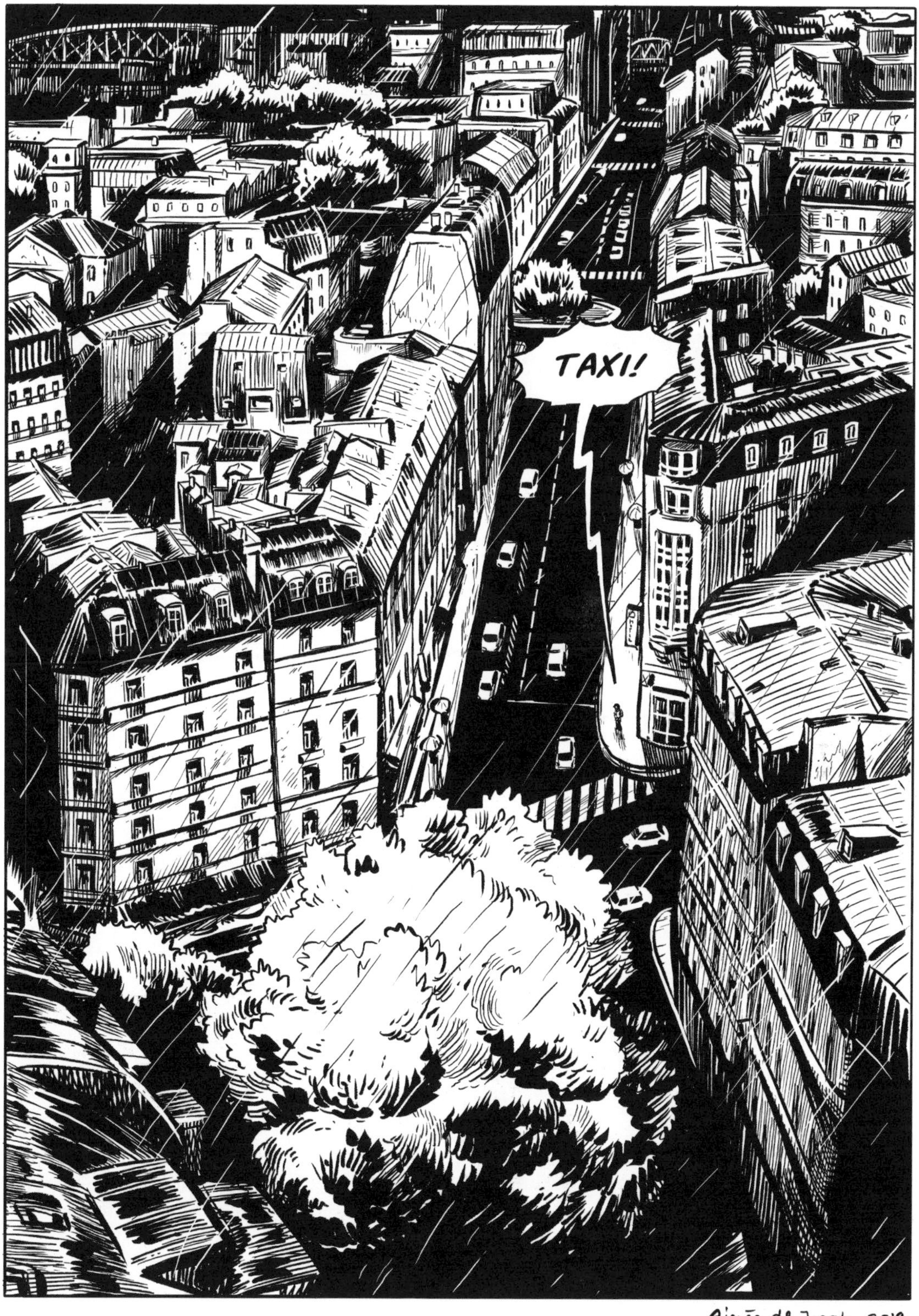
TAXI!

Aimée de Jongh, 2019

Washington Flyer Taxi
Dulles Int'l Airport
706-853-6094

Cab# 550

9/14/2017 6:41:02 PM

TRIP ID: 8898597
START: 9/14/2017 5:29:40 PM
END: 9/14/2017 6:39:08 PM
DISTANCE: 26.5 mi

                                  $67.22
                                   $0.00
                                   $2.65
Fare $4.00
Extras   Fee $69.87

epilogue

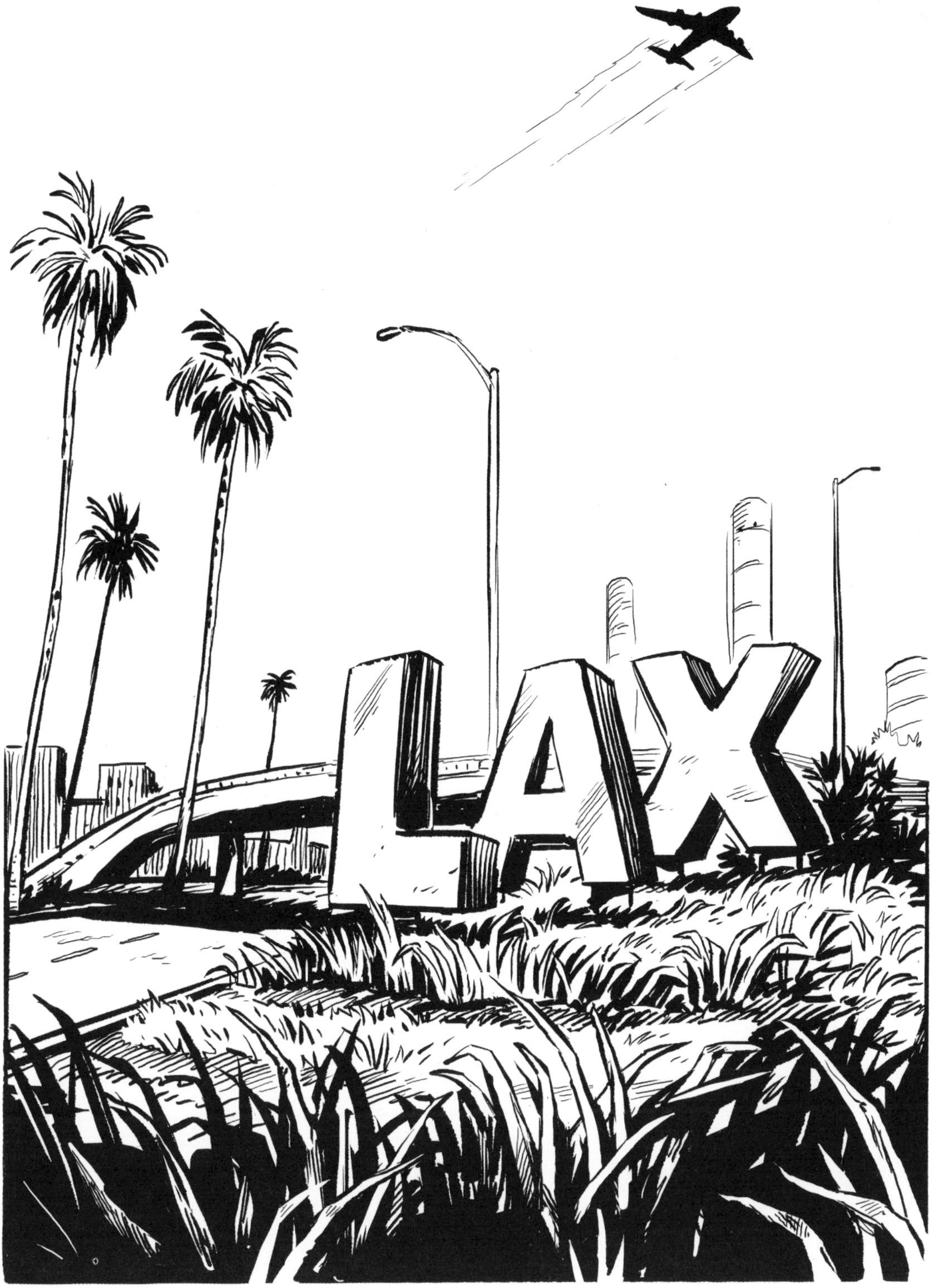
LAX

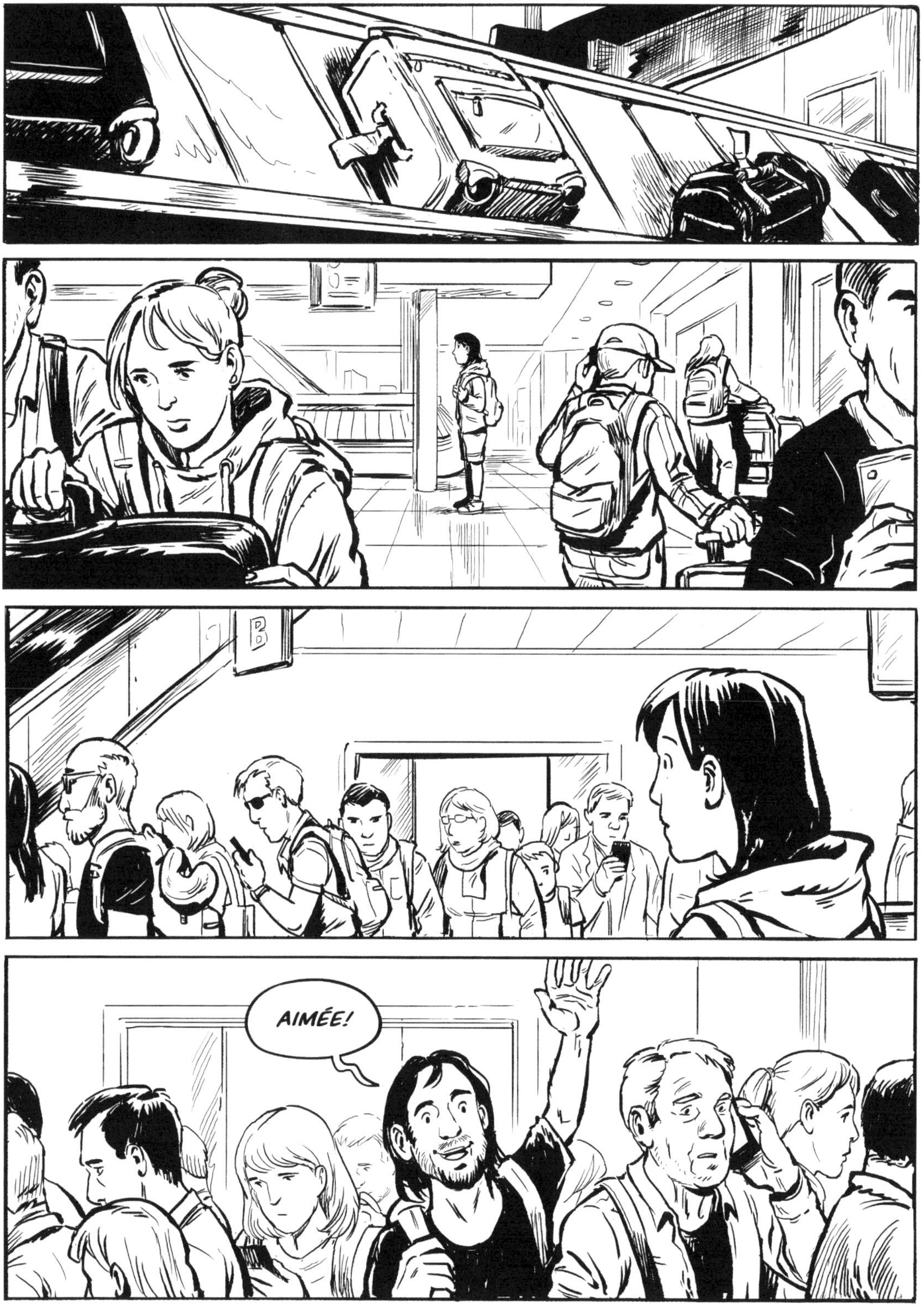
AIMÉE!

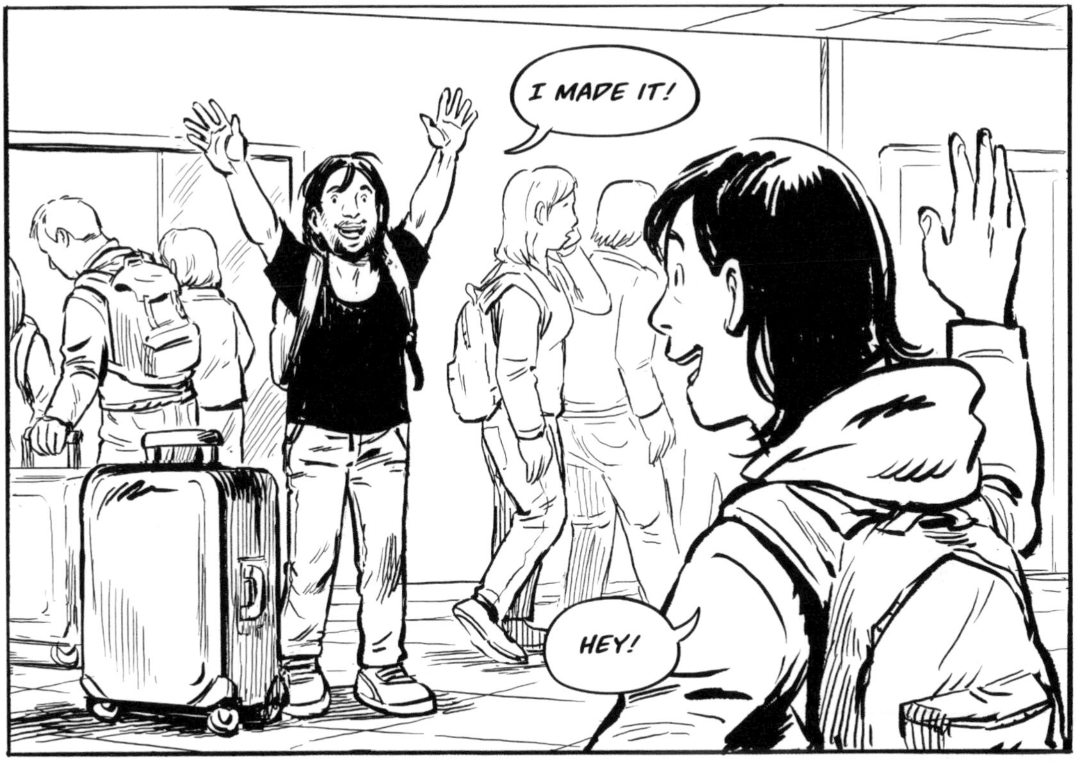
I MADE IT!
HEY!

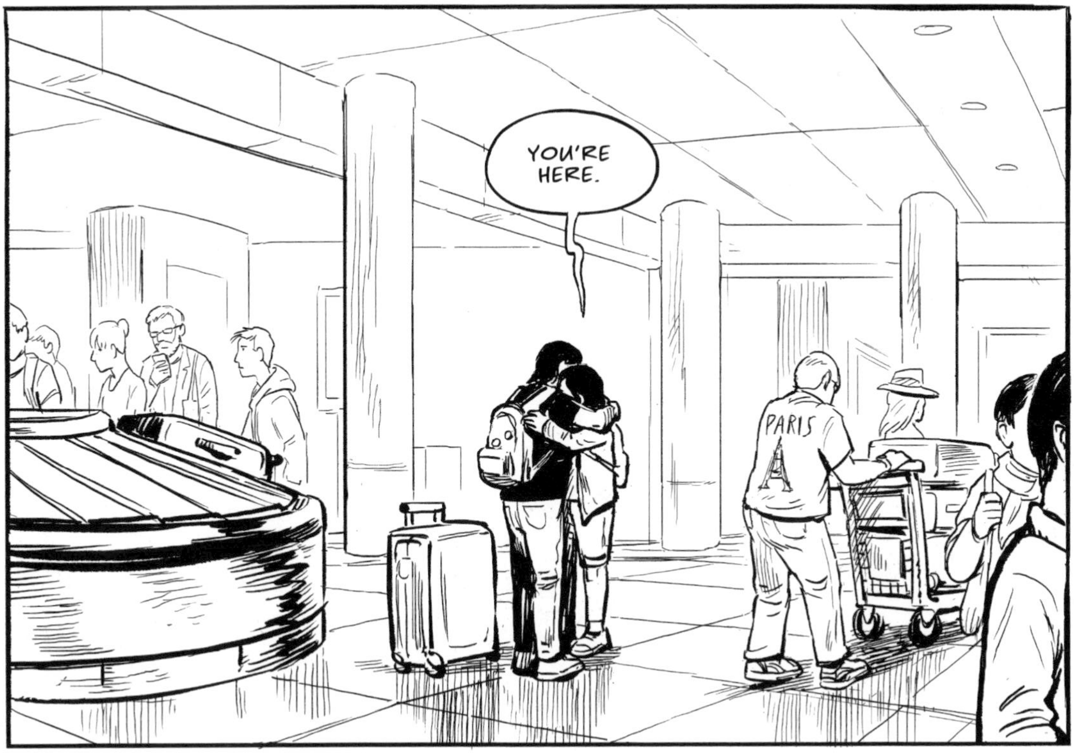
YOU'RE HERE.
PARIS

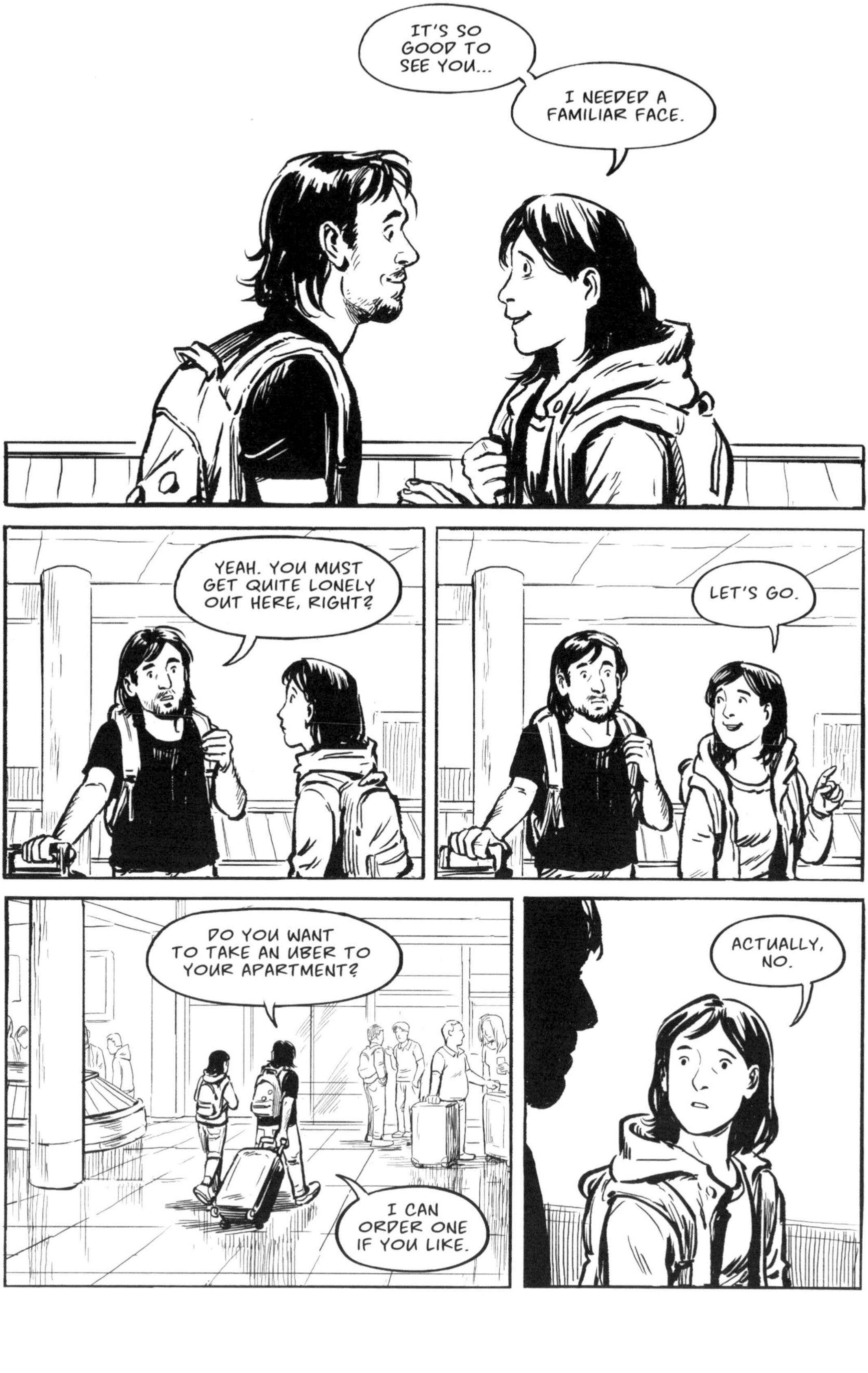
IT'S SO GOOD TO SEE YOU...
I NEEDED A FAMILIAR FACE.
YEAH. YOU MUST GET QUITE LONELY OUT HERE, RIGHT?
LET'S GO.
DO YOU WANT TO TAKE AN UBER TO YOUR APARTMENT?
I CAN ORDER ONE IF YOU LIKE.
ACTUALLY, NO.

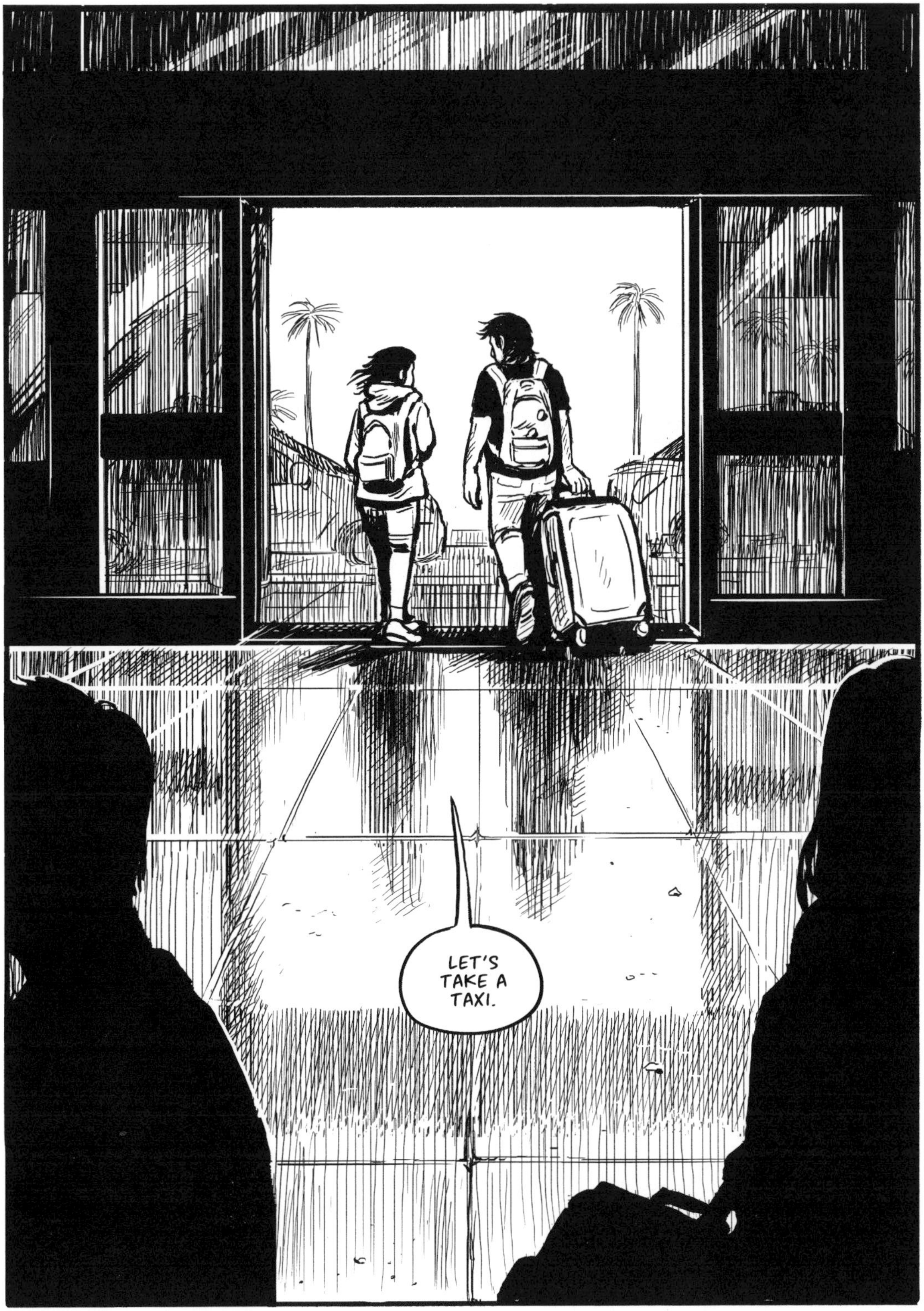
LET'S TAKE A TAXI.

Los Angeles, 2014

Aimée de Jongh (1988) has drawn comics from a very early age. After releasing her first book at age 17, she continued as a professional comic author and animator. Her work includes several animated films, a daily comic strip and two prize-winning graphic novels. After releasing her graphic novel *The Return of the Honey Buzzard*, Aimée was able to start a career outside of her home country the Netherlands. With all the travelling came lots of taxi rides, which have lead to the graphic memoir that you're holding right now.

Aimée lives and works in Rotterdam, the Netherlands.